CONVERTIBLES

CONVE

IAN KUAH

RTIBLES

SMITHMARK

A SALAMANDER BOOK

This edition published in 1993 by SMITHMARK Publishers Inc.,
16 East 32nd Street, New York, New York 10016

1 2 3 4 5 6 7 8 9

SMITHMARK books are available for bulk purchase for sales promotion and
premium use. For details write or call the manager of special sales,
SMITHMARK Publishers Inc., 16 East 32nd Street, New York,
NY 10016; (212) 532-6600

© Salamander Books Ltd, 1993

ISBN 0 8317 1797 1

All correspondence concerning the content of this book should be
addressed to Salamander Books Ltd, 129–137 York Way,
London N7 9LG, England

CREDITS

Editor: Richard Collins
Designer: Mark Holt
Filmset by Flair plan Photo-typesetting Ltd
Color reproduction P & W Graphics, Singapore
Printed in Italy

PHOTOGRAPHIC CREDITS

With the exception of the following, indicated by page numbers, all
photographs in this book were taken by Ian Kuah (© Ian Kuah): front
endpaper, Ian Dawson; 1, Mike Volanti; 2–3, Simon Childs; 4–5, 16–19,
32–5, *World Sports Cars*; 42–5, Tim Andrew; 46–9, Daniel B. Lyons; 50–55,
Garry Stuart (© Salamander Books Ltd); 60–65, Rick Graves; 70–73, Daniel
B. Lyons; 74–7, *Classic American*; 78–81 *World Sports Cars*; 108–113, Tim
Andrew; 128–31 *World Sports Cars*; 132–5, Simon Childs; back endpaper,
Garry Stuart (© Salamander Books Ltd). Unless otherwise stated, copyright for
all photographs is held by the above named.

ACKNOWLEDGMENTS

The author is grateful to the following for their help and cooperation in
supplying cars for photography: VW Golf GTI Cabriolet – Scotts of Sloane
Square, London; Ferrari Mondial Cabriolet – Steve Carter; Porsche 911
Cabriolet – Claire Knee, Porsche Cars GB Ltd, location courtesy of Guildford
Spectrum Leisure Complex; Lotus Elan SE – Patrick Peal, Lotus Cars Ltd,
locations courtesy of Brighton Palace Pier and The Royal Pavilion, Brighton;
Chevrolet Corvette – Chris Colbeck; additional thanks to Keith Beschi,
membership secretary Classic Corvette UK.

ADDITIONAL CAPTIONS

1 Alfa Romeo Spider; 2/3 TVR Griffith; 4/5 Honda Beat; front endpaper
Dodge Viper; back endpaper Chevrolet Corvette.

CONTENTS

A FOREWORD TO CONVERTIBLES

Driving open cars is a distressing, disgusting, disconcerting business. Only on one of those rare days when you have really hot sunshine above and a full gale following you from behind – no matter which way you turn – can you safely go out for some serious motoring without dressing up like a deep-sea diver. When the motoring is less serious, when you are in town confined by the dings and narrows of outrageous traffic, then your clothes are spattered and your lungs are ravaged by the grimy exhausts of those eye-watering diesels with which we are obliged to share the roads.

Only when speeds are relatively low (one may be quite serious about pottering) can open motoring be a kindly revelation. It is then that we remember the bliss of chuntering around the countryside in an open tourer with the canvas furled, the sidescreens stowed away and the windscreen folded flat. There is nothing, absolutely nothing, so conducive to a sense of being totally aware of the car and its environment as clear vision, unimpeded even by glass, through an azimuth of 360 mirror-aided degrees.

The ears appreciate surround-sound no less keenly. Those curiously wrought and variously fleshy flaps of the outer ears are quite miraculous in their direction-finding, and I remember with what discrimination they picked out the tock of a loose tappet in a Lancia Lambda, or the chitter of a stone trapped in the offside rear tread of a Morris 8. It was in the cars of that era, seldom fast enough to broach speed limits even as low as those so absurdly prevalent today, that the full joys of motoring without superstructure could be enjoyed. Only when the airspeed relative to the driver's nose is less than about 55mph can the sense of smell share the pleasure, noting the country fragrances of fern and hay and clover and silage, or recognizing the smell of London as one hits it after cresting the brow of the hill at Dunstable. On a frosty night it is the nose which senses the difference in those misty hollows where the ground temperature is likely to be freezing.

Les neiges d'antan? I remember driving from Hereford to North London in a New Year's Day blizzard so embracing that I never saw the road surface until I reached Northolt. In RAF greatcoat, balaclava and beret, augmented by some whacking great non-uniform guantlets, I had the windscreen and everything folded away and, without ever going terribly fast, made remarkable good time on the journey, overtaking everything in sight. At the time I believed, as was proper to my nineteen tender years, that it was because I was the only one who knew how to drive; I might now admit that it was probably because I was the only who could see where he was going.

Modern cars are really unsuitable for that sort of thing. They are, and have been for some time, too fast: I recall galumphing up the M1 in an early open E-Type Jaguar and finding that at 110mph I was so severely battered on the top of my head by the turbulence behind the windscreen that I had to slow down for fear of losing consciousness. Other chaps of shorter stature sat lower and further forward, suffered less and, presumably, went faster, though I never saw anybody do so. What I had to do was to erect the roof, after which I went *much* faster; and I must admit that the blinkering effect of a canvas awning does concentrate the mind upon the road ahead.

It would be nice to see it less massively framed, but modern legislation impedes the view. Today's car, being engineered for hitting concrete blocks or standing on its head rather than for clear-sighted driving, has to have a substantial frame all around its windscreen, another around each mirror, and as like as not there will be some supplementary bridgework behind the front seats – though not so far behind that a tall driver may not hit it with his head. That is how the targa-topped car came into being, the name having nothing to do with the shield-like properties of the detachable roof panel but deriving some sort of reflected glory from memories of the last of the great road races, the *Targa Florio*. It is not often that the Italian language has lent any of its beauty to the technical description of open bodywork. The *torpedo* body was what we generally described as an open tourer, but any self-respecting manufacturer might be shocked to learn that the Latin root was *torpere* – to be inactive. How it came about was that the crampfish, whose electrical discharges cause numbness in its enemy or prey, was called torpedo; the rest you can imagine.

Italians are fond of calling an open two-seater a spider, and the Germans are fond of spelling it Spyder. The word itself (related to spinning, but in the arachnid rather than in the motoring sense) comes from Old English, but in this context it was originally a spider phaeton, a sub-division of one of those many classes of bodywork to which the carriagebuilders of France applied their Gallic enthusiasm for logical classification. Thus a *coupé* was a vehicle that had been cut, though it might as readily have been cut short as cut down; if it had winding side-windows in its two doors and a soft folding roof, it was a drophead *coupé*, but if it also had side windows behind the B-posts (whether or not it had four doors) it was a *cabriolet*. If the front of the roof could be rolled back as far as the B-post, that did not make it a *coupé de ville*, for that had to be a vehicle with a short closed compartment for the brocaded rear-seat passengers while in liveried isolation the hired hands, the chauffeur and in the best-regulated households a footman, sat roofless in front. A saloon *de ville* was more expansive, but there might be a good case for arguing that it was a brougham – not to be confused with a *Landau,* nor with the *Landaulet* which some early Americans thought was a car with a folding top over the rear seats and nothing over the driver.

It was all much too confusing, especially for those Americans who never dreamed that their familiar cabs derived their name from England's taxicab or *taximeter cabriolet*. The Land of the Free never had much time for foreign languages, nor much time for complicating its own, but it did have an abiding and amazingly practical commitment to the automobile as part of its way of life.

No wonder that it was from the USA that the word *convertible* acquired its motoring usage. What could be simpler or clearer? A convertible automobile, like convertible currency, was simply something that, whatever it was, could be converted into something else – not gold, perhaps, but definitely something alluring.

It is that allure which Ian Kuah has captured in this book. Most, if not all, of his chosen specimens appeal to an irrational sense of something lost but ever enticing, the snows of yesteryear sought in the sunshine of tomorrow. I have not driven all of them, but I have driven more than enough of them, thank you very much; and if any one theme links them all in my mind, it is that the absence of a roof does not make a car good, nor make a good car bad. A 246 Dino, even though it be the Spider version, is still a little jewel; a Cobra, even with a hardtop superimposed, is still a frightfully inept substitute for a good motorcycle.

There is greater freedom of headgear when driving an open car. Indeed, there was a time when the use of one was synonymous with the wearing of funny hats.

Yet I cannot entirely quell a suspicion that the Caterham would be gorgeous as a close-coupled closed *coupé*, perhaps a little like the rare body that I once saw on a low-chassis 4.5-liter Invicta. It was in the normal open version of that wonderfully handsome old car that I first experienced the phenomenon of drowning in air, when the speed of the unimpeded blast striking one's face causes the flow to stall so that the nose is surrounded by a low-pressure area. It was like trying to breathe in a vacuum: I reached for my bowler hat, buried my face in it for a moment, and all was well; but it must have looked very odd, somewhat like Addison's de Coverley churchmate praying into his hat.

Sauce for the Caterham gander might also add savour to the Morgan goose. That was a car in which the effective maximum speed was determined by the backdraft lifting my beard in front of my face until it obscured my vision. There is an interesting comparative study in aerodynamics to be done here, for my beard rose only to the horizontal in that excellent car the BMW Z1 which, I am relieved to find, pleased Mr Kuah almost as much as it delighted me. Relieved, but hardly surprised: on those occasions when we have driven together, it has been reassuring to find that our views on what is good in cars correspond fairly well. In the confidence bred of that experience, I commend this book to you.

L.J.K. Setright

INTRODUCTION

Mankind really is quite perverse. On the one hand, he spends huge amounts of time and money trying to eradicate vestigial traces of the outside world from his motorcars with double glazing, insulation felt and complex rubber seals, while on the other he proliferates the concept of closeness to nature with open-topped cars. But open cars are not just about fresh air, they are also about individuality and freedom. And if they are two-seater sports car, they also inspire more emotional response in people of all ages from all walks of life than any other type of car. But the practical considerations of modern living demand that we sometimes carry more than two people in a vehicle. Thus, four-seater convertibles, based on saloons or hatchbacks, have become significant models in most major manufacturers' model ranges. It would have been very easy to add to the huge collection of existing books on classic cars that just happen to have rag-tops, but there is now a very well defined path of evolution taking place arguably because of and in spite of the plethora of similar looking computer generated designs. Call it escapism, conscious or otherwise, but like the character in that cult TV series 'The Prisoner', with his Lotus Seven, as we head for the turn of the twentieth century we need to flee the mundane sometimes just to keep our sanity. 1930s classics attract many people for their period elegance, their individuality compared to modern machinery and also the directness of their driving experience. But what can discourage buyers is the high prices of originals, the availability of parts and the amount of maintenance that cars of this era require. Thus, exquisite replicas like the De la Chapelle Bugatti T55 (p.56) which uses modern BMW mechanicals become attractive propositions. And if you are prepared to join a seven-year waiting list or buy pre-owned, living nostalgia in an even purer form can be had with a Morgan Plus 8 (p.114). Much the same can

be said for the smooth bodied cars of the 1950s and 1960s. Replicas of the Le Mans winning D-Type Jaguar and its XK-SS road car sister (p.92) are plentiful, but the Lynx replica is surely the finest made and is in some ways better than the original. Cars like this and the IAD-made Pegaso Z-103 (p.118) which have official sanction from their original manufacturers could even be referred to as evolution cars. This is because if they had stayed in production, the changes and updates made could well have been along such lines.

The AC Cobra (p.10) was the architypal 1960s muscle-bound sports car and is the most replicated car in history. It is also the only one where the original is still in production as well. The fabulous 1960s also saw the birth of another contemporary classic, the Alfa Romeo Spider (p.16) which was swept to immortality in the film, *The Graduate*. These and other elegant and curvacious sports cars were the inspiration for Peter Lorenz when he penned his stunning Silver Falcon (p.88) twenty years later.

If European convertibles tended to be mostly compact sports cars in the 1950s and 1960s, this was not the case in the United States. The two-seaters made there like the Corvette (p.50) and Thunderbird (p.74) were anything but small by European standards and got even bigger and took on rear seats in the late 1950s as marketing trends changed. American convertibles did not quite recover from excess flab and glitz until Ford launched the Mustang (p.70).

The threat of impending American roll-over legislation put the skids under so many promising open cars designed during the 1970s. The fallout from this was that cars like the Jaguar XJS and Triumph TR7 acquired ungainly fixed roofs. The collateral damage lasted years. British sports cars made by the volume were allowed to run until they were no longer economical to make, due to falling sales. The falling sales were caused by lack of investment in new product, something the Japanese, who swept up the market, could not be accused of. And the Japanese did it again in 1989 with the Mazda MX-5 Miata which kicked the complacent European car makers into touch once again. Only the smaller specialist manufacturers in Britain had not been sleeping, and excellent cars like the Lotus Elan (p. 96) were born.

But the timing was bad. As the boom of the 1980s turned to bust, even small, relatively inexpensive sports cars like the Mazda MX-5 Miata (p.102) and Lotus Elan languished in their showrooms as caution became the economic watchword all over the world.

These small and light cars are right not just for our times but for our environment. They do not eat up too much of our resources or take up too much roadspace, while their relative lack of mass gives them superior all-round dynamic abilities.

If small is beautiful, the Honda Beat (p.78), a Japanese home market model which has been widely personally imported into Europe, is the epitome of a small and agile fun car that puts a broad grin on its driver's face. The Beat is a direct descendant of the Honda S600 and S800 sports cars from the 1960s.

Having fun in an open car is possible at moderate speeds if a car is tactile and responsive enough, and the revival of the 1960s Austin Healey 'Frogeye' Sprite (p.20) by The Frogeye Car Company is living and buoyant testimony to this.

But power is addictive and the new wave of small sports cars with very powerful engines is seriously challenging the existence of the huge lumbering monsters like the Ferrari 512TR, Lamborghini Diablo and Jaguar XJ220. The Caterham HPC (p.36) is one car which will drive away from any big supercar down a twisty road. There is, however, a place for practical supercars, ones that can carry two people and their luggage across continents. A good example of this is Robert Jankel's Corvette-based Tempest (p.82) which offers Ferrari F40 performance in a user-friendly package for less than half the price. Less practical but equally exciting and even cheaper is the stunning Dodge Viper (p.60) which is a targa design.

Just the name Ferrari is emotive. But the most underrated Ferrari is one of the best. Apart from being cheaper than its 348 sister, the Mondial (p.66) has much more user-friendly handling. The Cabriolet version seats four and even has a reasonable trunk. Luggage space is limited in a Porsche 911's (p.122) front compartment, but the fold-down rear seats are better for luggage than carrying people anyway. The charismatic 911 celebrated its thirtieth anniversary in 1993 and its concept seems set to go on forever.

The world's most exclusive and expensive cars have traditionally been convertibles and, in yesteryear, the names to look for were Bugatti and Rolls-Royce. Today, the only cars that can outpoint the Mercedes SL (p.108) for status come from the stables of Rolls-Royce (p.128) and indeed Bentley. These hand-built cars offer the finest traditions of English craftsmanship together with an air of tranquil elegance unrivaled by the cars of any other nation.

TVR's sensational Griffith (p.132) is an up-to-the-minute interpretation of the traditional sports car with its front-engined, rear-wheel-drive layout while the BMW Z1 (p.26) shows a staggering amount of original thinking in its mid-front-engine layout, suspension design, drop-down doors and modular body construction.

We will always have and need practical four-seater open cars like the Golf GTI Cabriolet (p.140) and the BMW 325i Convertible (p.32), but the real open-air excitement lies with affordable and powerful sports cars like the Griffith and the Z1. Whether the traditional or the avante garde becomes the norm in the years to come is anybody's guess but, either way, the future of the convertible seems assured.

AC COBRA

If imitation is the sincerest form of flattery, then the AC Cobra must be the
most flattered car in automotive history. No other car has ever
spawned so many copies, some of which even use the same
engine as the original. The outstanding competition success
of the Cobra of the 1960s tends to overshadow the fact that it is the
product of Britain's oldest car company, which has operated
without a break from the day it was founded in 1901. Since 1992, Brian
Angliss has been the sole proprietor.

SPECIFICATION

Engine: Longitudinal, front, rear-wheel drive **Capacity:** 5.0 liter, 302cu.in. V8
Bore/stroke: 101.6 × 76.2mm **Power (DIN/rpm):** 320bhp @ 4750rpm **Torque (DIN/rpm):** 330lb ft @ 3750rpm
Fuel system/ignition: Holley 4-barrel, 780 CFM carburetor/electronic **Transmission:** 5-speed manual Borg Warner T50D
Front suspension: Independent by unequal length wishbones, coil springs, concentric Koni dampers
Rear suspension: Independent by unequal length wishbones, coil springs, concentric Koni dampers
Brakes: Four-wheel disc brakes ventilated at front **Wheels/tires:** Alloy. 7.5J × 15in. (F), 9.5J × 15in. (R);
225/65VR15 (F), 275/55VR15 (R). Pirelli P7R **Max. speed:** 150mph+ (241kph) **0–60mph:** 4.2 sec

Today's AC Cobra still uses all the original tooling in its manufacture. But subtle changes to the suspension make it more user friendly. The current lightweight Cobra is also the fastest accelerating road version, establishing official 0–60mph (0–96kph) and 0–100mph (0–160kph) times of 4.27 and 10.0 seconds respectively in late 1992 with full EC emission controls in place.

The Cobra story began in 1961 when Texan race driver, Carroll Shelby, with the backing of the Ford Motor Company, entered negotiations with AC Cars to install a Ford V8 engine in the lightweight AC Ace. This trans-Atlantic liaison gave birth to one of the fastest sports cars of

all time and a legend that will run for as long as people love cars. In 1963, a pair of 289 Cobras contested the Le Mans 24-Hour race and one of them was the first British car to finish. The later 427 Cobra had a listing in the *Guinness Book of Records* as the world's fastest production car and works Cobras won the Sports Car World Championship in 1965.

The early narrow bodied 289 Cobra was named after its 289cu. in. (4.7 liter) V8 engine. With the original suspension, handling and grip were marginal. So when Shelby decided to drop the 427cu. in. (7.0 liter) motor into the Cobra in 1964 to trounce Ferrari on the track, a new chassis was developed. Using early computers, Shelby and Ford designed the ultimate tubular chassis and four-link suspension of their day to handle the 490bhp and near 500lb ft of torque of the race-tuned 427cu. in. engine. With its engine sitting far back in the chassis, today's 302cu. in. (5.0 liter) lightweight Cobra has a 50/50 weight distribution.

The quality of the hand-beaten aluminum bodywork is simply stunning and the chromework is mirror-fine. Climb in, and you are greeted by painstakingly finished leatherwork with perfect stitching. Even the 'string' you pull to open the door is actually a thong of leather that has been lovingly shaped and finished to serve a utilitarian purpose below its noble character. The big V8 starts up like rolling thunder, especially in a confined space. The clutch is heavy but progressive; just a tad of throttle as it engages smoothly and the Cobra trundles forward, its two big stainless steel exhaust pipes burbling away. Give the car its head on the open road and the V8 burble changes to an awe-inspiring ripping, woofling growl accompanied by an unrelenting wave of torque. The sound and the push in the back rise together as if choreographed and by the time you approach the red line on the tacho, the four-barrel Holley carburetor is sucking for all its worth, the roar of the twin exhausts has built to a crescendo, and it is time for the next gear. Slow in, fast out is the order of the day in bends. The messages from the Cobra's helm eloquently describe what the front wheels are doing.

The sensuous aluminum body of the AC Cobra is the aesthetic pinnacle of the compound curve on wheels. Combined with the thunder of a big American V8 engine, it conjures up the most stirring image on earth. Three decades on, the draw of motoring's greatest sports car legend shows no sign of waning.

14

ALFA ROMEO SPIDER

The Alfa Romeo Spider is one of Pininfarina's most enduring shapes.
From its sleek pointed nose to its recently restyled
Kamm-tail, the Spider exudes the Italian brio that made it such an
appropriate car for Dustin Hoffman to be seen driving
in the 1967 box-office hit, *The Graduate*. As with Hoffman,
looks alone did not win the day. But magnetic
personality in the car's instance comes from its classic
twin-cam engine.

SPECIFICATION

Engine: Longitudinal, front, rear-wheel drive **Capacity:** 1962cc, four cylinders in-line
Bore/stroke: 84 × 88.5mm **Power (DIN/rpm):** 120bhp @ 5800rpm **Torque (DIN/rpm):** 118lb ft @ 4200rpm
Fuel system/ignition: Bosch Motronic injection/electronic ignition **Transmission:** 5-speed manual
Front suspension: Wishbone, coil springs, anti-roll bar
Rear suspension: Live axle, trailing arms, coil springs, anti-roll bar
Brakes: Four-wheel disc **Wheels/tires:** Alloy. 6J × 15in. 195/60HR15
Max. speed: 118mph (189kph) **0–60mph:** 9.4 sec

Over the years, the Alfa Spider has built up a large following the world over, and yet when it was launched at the 1966 Geneva Motor Show the motoring press had mixed feelings about its looks, saying that it lacked the finesse of Pininfarina's earlier Giuletta Spider. Nicknamed the 'boat-tail' because of the pointed rear which balanced its prow, the early Duetto took its styling cue from the 1950 Alfa show car appropriately dubbed the Disco Volante, or 'flying saucer'. Purity of line and detail was a strong point all the way from the Perspex headlamp covers to the chromed exhaust tail-pipe.

Equally astonishing was the performance. Aerodynamically efficient, the Alfa managed

105mph (168kph) from just 1590cc and 109bhp. More than that, the sound of its two Weber twin-choke carburetors breathing deeply as the engine revved smoothly to its 6000rpm red line was an orgasmic experience for *aficionados* of the marque. Two years later, capacity was increased to 1779cc, the car renamed the 1750 Spider and top speed shot up to a dramatic 118mph (189kph).

The purists who had originally quibbled over Pininfarina's styling had just got used to it when their sensibilities were dealt another blow. In 1970, The Spider had its boat-tail truncated to a Kamm-tail and it was not until the following year, when the car acquired a 1962cc engine to become the 2000 Spider Veloce, that the mutterings once again grew silent. As the era of safety and emissions loomed large on the horizon, the purity of line began to suffer. The Perspex headlamp covers were the first thing to go. They were not allowed in the USA right from the start and as politicians began to interfere in European markets too, Alfa Spiders around the world became more encumbered with things like impact fenders and fuel-injection. In fact, fuel-injection kept performance competitive in a world where emission laws had gained a stranglehold on engine outputs. In these early days, before the microchip age, it was the only way of keeping engines reasonably clean and smooth running. First, the car had Spica mechanical fuel-injection, followed in 1982 by Bosch L-Jetronic. 1990 cars onwards use Bosch Motronic injection and have just 120bhp and 118lb ft of torque.

After a couple of ham-fisted visual updates, however, the latest Spider has regained the clean and unencumbered look of the original 1966 Duetto. The new one-piece wraparound fenders are modern but merge harmoniously with the classic curves of Alfa. The thin linear tail-light strip is contemporary Alfa but works surprisingly well, actually giving the car a more cohesive rear-end. A very subtle ducktail spoiler is part of the sheetmetal and is an elegant touch. The updated design package has once again endowed the Spider with a coherent and purposeful look.

Driving the Spider is an idiosyncratic experience. The revised cabin has many new parts and yet so much is old. The newness is almost a veneer and you can tell when you begin to drive the car. The engine is more tractible than ever, but it is not lusty in the way that the original 2.0 liter carburetored car was. Moreover, the high rpm breathing of the engine now seems reined in, and does not sound as nice. The car's responses are still sharp compared to sterile modern saloons, but don't expect modern levels of roadholding. Unlike the Porsche 911 which has been comprehensively re-engineered over time, the Alfa Spider has benefitted only from cosmetic face-lifts to paper over the cracks. But take this roadster at face value, enjoy it for its style and unique Latin charm and you will not be disappointed.

AUSTIN HEALEY SPRITE

Sports cars are emotive. An expensive saloon will hardly rate
a second glance at your local watering hole, but
pull up in an immaculate sports car, especially a classic one, and
you can be sure of attracting interested and possibly
envious bystanders. The everlasting appeal of this particular
car – the Austin Healey 'Frogeye' Sprite – led an
Isle of Wight-based motor salvage specialist Keith Brading
to embark on the rebirth of this classic sports car in 1981.

SPECIFICATION

Engine: Longitudinal, front, rear-wheel drive **Capacity:** 1392cc, in-line four, SOHC
Bore/stroke: 77.24 × 74.3mm **Power (DIN/rpm):** 75bhp @ 5800rpm **Torque (DIN/rpm):** 80.5lb ft @ 4000rpm
Fuel system/ignition: One twin-choke downdraft carburetor/electronic ignition **Transmission:** 5-speed manual
Front suspension: Independent. Lever arm
Rear suspension: Live axle. Rubber-in-torsion trailing arm system. Telescopic dampers
Brakes: Front discs, rear drums **Wheels/tires:** Alloy. 5J × 13in. 155/HR13
Max. speed: 110mph (176kph) **0–60mph:** 9.5 sec

Four years later, in 1985, the quaint little workshop just down the road from the Hoverport in Ryde flung open its doors and a rejuvenated version of the diminutive roadster with the smiling face spluttered and rasped its way into the world. But instead of a rot prone steel body, the new Frogeye wore a glass-fiber bodyshell around a fully galvanized steel chassis. And so the Frogeye Car Company was born.

Type approval was not a problem for these cars, as British law decrees that if the car retains the front chassis rail with its stamped-in chassis number from the original donor car, then the new vehicle is the original Healey Sprite, merely restored and updated. Purists of course bemoaned the passing of their rusty original cars, calling the GRP body a heresy. But official sanction from Geoffrey Healey, son of Donald Healey who designed the original, put paid to that argument very quickly. Brading could not have left the mechanicals of the Sprite alone

21

however, for by today's standards the car is woefully underpowered and the handling inept. The original Frogeye used a 1.0 liter BMC A-Series engine and Brading chose the 1275cc version of the same unit for the heart of his Frogeye, but in the form of a reconditioned, overbored 1293cc unit good for 65bhp and 72lb ft of torque.

However, demand from export markets has now necessitated a change of power unit to meet the emission regulations in markets like Germany where a catalytic convertor is mandatory. At the same time, donor cars have become scarce so that, even in the UK, all-new Frogeye replicas will have to meet the same EC-wide emission standards even if low volume type approval exempts them from other requirements. Thus, the latest production Frogeye uses a 73bhp Ford CVH 1.4 liter engine coupled to a Ford Sierra five-speed gearbox. This has made a substantial and positive difference to both acceleration and cruising ability, and thankfully retains a similar exhaust note.

The front suspension of the new Frogeye is the original independent wishbone, upper lever-arm shock and coil spring

design made from exchange parts. But the primitive cart-sprung rear axle has given way to a more sophisticated rubber-in-torsion bar system with trailing arm location and telescopic dampers. This new rear axle offers a better ride/handling compromise while retaining simplicity. Another new offering is the optional hardtop which turns the spartan but nicely trimmed interior into a cosy shelter from the elements.

Driving the Frogeye makes you realize that you do not need hundreds of horsepower to have fun. Coming out of bends, the light weight and good torque of the engine enable the car to gather speed briskly, and the high fifth gear makes all the difference to cruising. The wonderfully direct and communicative steering tells you exactly what is passing under the front wheels while the back axle can be felt wriggling its way over bumps; it is a total driving sensation.

The Japanese have tried with small sports cars like the Mazda MX-5, but it seems that at the end of the day it is impossible to copy certain characteristics of 1960s English sports cars. Perhaps they turn out this way because of the people who make them.

BMW Z1

In German, *Zukunft* means future, hence the 'Z' in the title of BMW's late eighties roadster. But the Z1 was really a back-to-the-future exercise for BMW, the Munich-based aero-engine manufacturer who spawned the 328, 503 and 507 two-seaters from the 1940s to the 1960s. After running into financial trouble, the company was saved by a succession of high performance saloons that changed its direction and its fortunes. And in 1989 it ended a twenty-five year absence from the sports car scene with the Z1.

SPECIFICATION

Engine: Longitudinal, front, rear-wheel drive **Capacity:** 2494cc, in-line six
Bore/stroke: 84 × 75mm **Power (DIN/rpm):** 170bhp @ 5800rpm **Torque (DIN/rpm):** 167lb ft @ 4000rpm
Fuel system/ignition: Bosch Motronic/electronic **Transmission:** 5-speed manual
Front suspension: Independent. MacPherson strut, coil springs, anti-dive geometry
Rear suspension: Independent. Central arm axle, longitudinal control arm, double track control arm, anti-squat, anti-dive
Brakes: Four-wheel disc. Vented front **Wheels/tires:** Alloy. 7.5J × 16in. 225/45VR16
Max. speed: 135mph (217kph) **0–60mph:** 7.9 sec

The first complete project of BMW's advanced design and engineering division, Technik GmbH, the brain-storming, lateral-thinking counterpart of BMW Motorsport, the Z1 was first shown as a prototype in 1986. Using the 325i engine as its starting point, Technik clothed an immensely strong combination backbone and perimeter steel skeleton with an all-plastic bodyshell.

Comprising thirteen clip-on panels with a deformable nose-cone, the modular bodywork simplifies accident repairs and lowers the potential cost of updating the styling. It was even suggested at one point that an owner could have a set of different colored panels for a change of 'clothing' to suit a different mood or season!

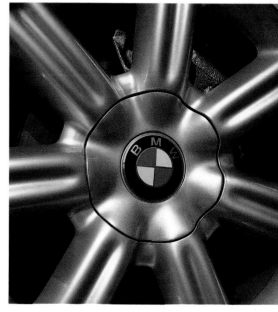

Clever design features abound. Operated by a pair of motors, the doors drop vertically into the deep sills for access or for a greater sense of the great outdoors. Press the lock button or pull the inside handle again to reverse the process. Under the stubby Kamm tail is a 'missing' panel which vents airflow from the aerofoil shaped transverse exhaust silencer box. This arrangement splits the underbody airflow to create stabilizing negative lift at the rear.

In catalysed form, the 2.5 liter straight-six engine produces 170bhp at 5800rpm and 167lb ft of torque at 4000rpm. Sited well back in the chassis the engine helps create a weight distribution of 49/51 in what BMW term a 'front-mid-engined car'. The front suspension comes from the E30 BMW 325i but the rear is a multi-link design that BMW call a centrally guided, spherical double wishbone axle. It is, in effect, a suspension system with anti-dive and anti-squat

properties which maintains geometric accuracy in all movement planes.

The cabin is simple and neat, with moulded plastic bucket seats covered by foam-filled, patterned leather-trimmed cushions. These look hard but are in fact supremely comfortable and supportive.

Capable of pulling 1g lateral acceleration in a turn, the Z1 is brisk rather than lightning quick in a straight line. The 12-valve 2.5 liter engine is not reknowned for good low speed torque and this is compounded by the car weighing 200lb more than the 325i. Thus, 0–60mph (0–96kph) takes 7.9 seconds and top speed is 135mph (217kph). The Z1 is not unusually efficient aerodynamically, but its Cd of 0.36 top up and 0.43 top down are not bad figures by open car standards.

If the weather should turn, the top can be up in a jiffy. As with the 325i convertible, you simply pop open the hinged rear deck panel, whip the canvas top up, secure it in front and drop the lid again to be cossetted in a snug and dry environment. The Z1 succeeds through its collective strengths. It looks different – and good. It has a robust and smooth engine, terrific grip and handling, well damped ride, and light and progressive controls. Eight thousand Z1s were built in left-hand drive only, on the old pilot production line at Munich between 1988 and 1990, so they are rare. The shape should still look good in the year 2000, the zinc-coated chassis and plastic body ensuring that the cars survive the ravages of time. But with qualities that reach far beyond its petite looks, the Z1 is a car you have to live with to realize that its charm is of the intelligent rather than the charismatic kind.

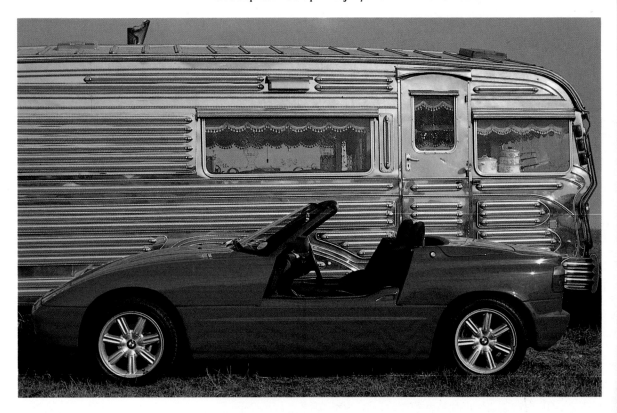

BMW 325i CONVERTIBLE

The BMW 3-series Convertible is the car that owners of VW Golf and Ford Escort Cabriolets aspire to. Among the youthful and upwardly mobile from Los Angeles to Tokyo, the open BMW is a symbol of quality, achievement and freedom. BMW briefly made a 1602 convertible in the late 1960s, before pursuing the safer route of the cabriolet with its integral roll-over bar. True al fresco motoring did not return to BMW until 1986 when the E-30 3-Series Convertible was launched.

SPECIFICATION

Engine: Longitudinal, front, rear-wheel drive **Capacity:** 2494cc, in-line six, four valves/cylinder
Bore/stroke: 84 × 75mm **Power (DIN/rpm):** 192bhp @ 5900rpm **Torque (DIN/rpm):** 181lb ft @ 4200rpm
Fuel system/ignition: Bosch Motronic/electronic **Transmission:** 5-speed manual/5-speed automatic
Front suspension: MacPherson strut, coil springs, anti-dive geometry
Rear suspension: Central arm axle, longitudinal control arm, double track control arm, anti-squat, anti-dive
Brakes: Four-wheel disc. Vented front. ABS **Wheels/tires:** Alloy. 7J × 15in. 205/60VR15
Max. speed: 143mph (230kph) **0–60mph:** 8.4 sec

It was obviously what the people had been waiting for, as the car was an instant and ongoing sales success. By the time production ended in late 1992, 140,000 cars had been sold, far exceeding anticipated sales projections. The E-36 Convertible, launched in the summer of 1993, was the third bodyshell variant of the compact luxury saloon and coupé which has set the class handling and safety standards. The 3-Series convertible comes with a host of active and passive safety features like ABS, drivers' airbag, seat-belt tensioners and retainers and a windscreen frame that will withstand one and a half times the weight of the car. An option is a rear roll-bar system that springs into position if the car is about to turn over. Both this and the steering wheel airbag can be retro-fitted, an industry first. Part of the design brief, all these safety features are neatly integrated into the car and are not noticed until they are deployed. Although the Convertible is very distinctly 3-Series, the body line is level with the door's upper edge and thus lower than the coupé's from which it is derived. This gives the topless version a flat rather than wedge-shaped look, which helps to accentuate its length.

Car manufacturers have always struggled to make their convertibles look good with the top up. BMW designers worked hard on this one as the 3-Series is a car that can be driven all year round. A development of the power-top on its predecessor, the new lined top folds elegantly with the aid of electro-hydraulics in

about 30 seconds into its covered compartment behind the rear seat. The process of locking and unlocking is made easy by a central twist-grip lever and a single button allows all the windows to be opened or closed at once. Another convenience is a facility that automatically lowers the windows by 0.6 inches so that you don't need to drop the glass slightly before raising the top.

Using the latest specification 24-valve straight-six engine with variable valve timing for better low-end torque, the 325i Convertible has 192bhp at 5900rpm and 181lb ft of torque at 4200rpm. But with all its structural strengthening, the 264lb heavier Convertible is not as swift through the gears as its saloon and coupé sisters. Even so, a 0–60mph (0–96kph) time of 8.4 seconds and a top speed of 143mph (230kph) are not to be sniffed at.

With a 50/50 weight distribution and a rear axle derived from the BMW Z1

sports car, the 325i Convertible handles and rides very well and, even on the sinuous and undulating French mountain roads where BMW launched the car, the bodyshell felt tight and rattle free even if the odd bit of plastic trim in the back occasionally protested. It was really only on steep inclines that the extra weight of the open version noticeably blunted the torque gains of the new engine. Cruising on the French autoroutes or just cantering down the seafront between Nice and Monte Carlo, the straight-six engine was always a paradigm of smoothness.

The BMW 325i Cabriolet is a car for all seasons. It has the chic and elegance you need to roll up to any occasion, while it has the interior and trunk space for four to embark on a long trip. It also provides cosy protection when the sun stops shining. And if you should need all the practical attributes of this car *sans* power, a 318i four cylinder version is also available.

CATERHAM SUPER SEVEN HPC

When Colin Chapman said, 'It is easy to make a bridge stand, difficult to make it just stand', he was referring to the fine balancing act between durability and speed that gave his Lotus Super Seven its fabulous power-to-weight ratio. Nearly three decades on, Caterham's Super Seven has taken the design philosophy of its progenitor to an all-time high. A good power-to-weight ratio gives lively acceleration but as kinetic energy increases with the square of speed, light weight also brings superior handling and braking.

SPECIFICATION

Engine: Longitudinal, front, rear-wheel drive **Capacity:** 1998cc, in-line four
Bore/stroke: 86 × 86mm **Power (DIN/rpm):** 175bhp @ 6000rpm **Torque (DIN/rpm):** 155lb ft @ 4800rpm
Fuel system/ignition: 2 twin-choke Weber 45DCOE carburetors/mapped electronic **Transmission:** 5-speed manual
Front suspension: Double wishbone, unequal length. Bilstein dampers, anti-roll bar
Rear suspension: Trailing arms, Bilstein dampers, anti-roll bar
Brakes: Four-wheel disc **Wheels/tires:** Alloy. 7J × 16in. 205/45ZR16 Goodyear GS-D
Max. speed: 126mph (202kph) **0–60mph:** 5.2 sec

The Caterham HPC, today's ultimate production expression of the original concept, has twice the engine capacity and nearly thrice the power of Colin Chapman's Lotus, but it is not significantly heavier. It is, however, significantly stronger. Using computer aided design for structural optimization, the Caterham's chassis is three times stiffer than the original while composite materials like honeycombed aluminum in strategic parts of the bodywork make it an infinitely safer car in an accident.

Another area where great strides have been made is in the suspension. The de Dion rear axle was introduced in 1985, but more recently extensive work with Bilstein on the suspension has resulted in a

car that not only handles better but also rides remarkably well. The handling bias can be adjusted via a four-position rear anti-roll bar which allows you to dial in more oversteer so you can enjoy the handling at reasonable speeds or more stabilizing understeer for race track work. The elemental lightness in the car's design permeates just about every detail. It would have been easy for Caterham to use proprietary alloy wheels for instance. Instead, they got GKN Alloys to make special five-spoke wheels designed to take the relatively light loadings of the Caterham. At just 6.7kg (15lb) each, they are about 40 percent lighter than a wheel for a mid-sized family hatchback.

Power comes from a modified version of the Vauxhall/Opel 2.0 liter 16-valve engine. Developed for Caterham by Langford & Peck, the engine had its Bosch fuel-injection system supplanted by a pair of traditional Weber carburetors. Caterham's technical director, Jez Coates, explains that 'the trouble-free and effective injection system

would not fit under the bonnet line and our customers would not have condoned the loss of the sucking and gurgling sounds that a tuned Caterham makes!'.

With a pair of Weber 45DCOEs, output is 175bhp in road trim, a significant 25bhp above the catalysed fuel-injected engines. With Weber 48DCOEs in race trim, a further 15bhp can be found and in extended testing with different cams and exhaust, Caterham have squeezed 230bhp from an HPC engine.

Feel and sound is what the car is all about. The steering is quick, positive and full of information. The brakes require a firm push but you know what they are doing and they work well. The stubby four-inch high gear lever does its job with a solid and positive feel while even the clutch pedal is a progressive instrument that talks you through each half-inch of its travel. In full cry, the Caterham is a cacophony of mechanical noises. Accelerate firmly, and the bark of the exhaust follows a nanosecond behind the thunderous roar of the twin-cam picking up, its four induction throats inhaling hard. All the way, wind noise increases to a frenzy as the 0.6 plus drag coefficient slams the car into an ever deepening wall of air. Like kinetic energy, drag also increases with the square of speed, so at 120mph the little car is still two grand short of its 7500rpm rev limiter.

The HPC is not about flat out highway cruising, but with its ride and handling elevated to an all-time high, the HPC really is the quintessential driver's sports car.

CADILLAC ALLANTE

Automotive history has recorded great distances being covered by coachbuilt bodies to mate them with their mechanicals. As recently as 1992, Zagato-built aluminum body-shells recreated the journey from Italy to England of the original Aston Martin DB4GT Zagatos when four Sanction 2 cars were made on leftover chassis. But no such liaison has ever spanned the distance of the Turin–Detroit airbridge established to build the Cadillac Allante.

SPECIFICATION

Engine: Longitudinal, front, rear-wheel drive **Capacity:** 4565cc, V8 (1993 spec, Northstar engine) DOHC, four valves/cylinder
Bore/stroke: N/A **Power (DIN/rpm):** 299bhp **Torque (DIN/rpm):** 291lb ft
Fuel system/ignition: Electronic fuel-injection/ignition **Transmission:** 4-speed automatic
Front suspension: MacPherson strut, lateral arm, oscillating arm, anti-roll bar
Rear suspension: MacPherson strut, transverse leaf spring, H-control arm
Brakes: Four-wheel disc. Bosch. ABS **Wheels/tires:** Alloy. 7J × 15in. 225/60VR15
Max. speed: 140mph (225kph) **0–60mph:** 7.0 sec

The working relationship between Pininfarina and Cadillac was not unprecedented. Even before the Italian firm took on its present title, bodymaker Battista (Pinin)Farina, who had founded his company in 1930 at the age of thirty-seven, bodied a V16 Cadillac chassis for the Maharajah of Orchha a year later. In 1959, the company was asked to make 200 special Cadillac Broughams. Then at the 1982 Turin Show, Sergio Pininfarina was approached by three GM executives and asked if his company would like to build a two-seater coupé-convertible for Cadillac.

The concept of an American-European car could have thrown up a styling dichotomy,

but Pininfarina had very clear ideas about his solution: the lines of the car had to be pure Italian, simple and elegant. Only in the front grille and tail-light details does the Allante have strong American overtones and even then they have been skillfully integrated. Ingenuity is clear for instance where US legislation requires a third stop-light at the rear. That has been interpreted by making the third light circular and it incorporates both the trunk lock as well as the Cadillac emblem.

The Allante never really took off in sales terms. Cadillac admit to trying to woo a younger buyer than the over-fifties age group of their sedans. Despite a 55–65mph (88–104kph) speed limit in the US, it is what a car can do rather than what its driver might want to do that is important.

On the open road, the Allante is composed, capable and both rides and grips well. Its handling belies a 63/37 percent weight distribution thanks partly to the latest electronically modulated dampers that seem to have an instant answer to any road surface. Poise is this car's middle name.

More than just a styling exercise on crude American underpinnings, the Cadillac Allante is a thoroughly engineered car that provides a serious challenge to Europe's finest luxury tourers. After years of uninspired barges, the US auto industry has at last risen to the challenge from its European counterparts. The Cadillac Allante is the vanguard of a new generation of world-class Americans.

CADILLAC ELDORADO

It is a little-known fact that Cadillac, America's answer to Rolls-Royce, has a
competition history, and an illustrious one at that. But in fact
a stock 1950 Cadillac, driven by Sam and Miles Collier, was placed tenth
overall at Le Mans that year, while a tuned version driven by
Briggs Cunningham was even faster but finished eleventh after losing
its top gear. It may have looked big and bulky, but the
160bhp Cadillac was no slouch and could stay with the highly respected
Jaguar XK120 through the gears to 90mph!

SPECIFICATION
Engine: Longitudinal, front, rear-wheel drive **Capacity:** 331cu. in. OHV V8
Bore/stroke: 3.81 × 3.63in. **Power (DIN/rpm):** 230bhp **Torque (DIN/rpm):** N/A
Fuel system/ignition: Carburetor/mechanical **Transmission:** Hydra-Matic
Front suspension: Independent, coil springs, telescopic dampers
Rear suspension: Live axle, leaf springs, telescopic dampers
Brakes: Drums front and rear **Wheels/tires:** N/A
Max. speed: 115mph (185kph) **0–60mph:** 11.0 sec

Unlike Rolls-Royce though, Cadillac was not always king of the mountain. Until the mid-1940s, Packard was the name people looked to for luxury and status. But a combination of the depression the decade before and the contractions made during the war years was what really carved out the future fortunes of these two companies. Hard times meant that both had to turn to the manufacture of less ostentatious vehicles to stay afloat. After the war, Packard got stuck in the rut of producing volume middle-class cars while Cadillac took the opportunity to revert to making exclusively luxury cars.

More than just adopting the mantle of standard bearer of style, Cadillac also produced the under-pinnings to go with it. Their new overhead valve V8 engine launched in 1949 along with the Coupe de Ville, gave them an all-around edge. By 1952, Cadillac had won 80 percent of the luxury car market. The secret of Cadillac's success was to produce just a small range of cars and make them to the highest standards from the finest materials. Customers appreciated that. Visual trademarks of the new Cadillac were the huge chromed front grille and

fender, aptly nicknamed the 'dollar grin', while at the rear the upswept tail-fins produced a distinctive hind view. Another Caddy stamp established with this car was the dummy airscoop on the leading edge of each rear fender.

In the early 1950s, people were still very price conscious and the 1953 Cadillac Eldorado cost $7,750. Expensive. Only 532 were made. But further down the line, as times got better, the high price worked in its favor. Anyone who was anyone had a Cadillac Eldorado, and suddenly everyone else was willing to pay the price for entry to an exclusive club.

The 1954 model (shown here) was a significant car in Cadillac's history. It was the model that guaranteed Cadillac's long-running premier series in the model line-up. An attractive car in its own right, the '54 Caddy Eldorado combined the flair of the wide-line restyle with many special features exclusive to the Eldorado. By now, Cadillac was playing the marketing game well, and the price of the car was $5,738, $2,000 less than the '53 model. Still high for the times, it was not excessive when the cachet of the car was taken into account however, and sales were encouraging with 2,150 cars sold that year, double the figures of its nearest rival, the Buick Skylark.

The '54 Caddy was also the precursor to the later finned car that would replace it. It was eight inches longer overall with a three inch longer wheelbase than its predecessor, and handling was better thanks to a wider track frame with improved bracing and uprated engine, suspension and steering mounts and new angled telescopic dampers.

The 1954 Cadillac Eldorado was a significant car in the company's history. Built in smaller numbers than the other cars in the model line-up, it had a better reputation for quality. Despite being cheaper than the Seventy-Five, the Eldorado was recognized as the best car that Cadillac made in 1954.

CHEVROLET CORVETTE

Post-war America was boom time for the motor industry, and Detroit was turning
out dozens of concept cars at shows to whet the hungry appetites
of potential customers. But amid the throng of manufacturers, only General
Motors took the plunge and built a dream machine that you
could actually buy. Made from a new wonder material, glass-fiber,
the Chevrolet Corvette made its debut in 1953. The genesis of the
Corvette began in 1951 when GM design chief, Harley Earl, began to
map out his ideas for a two-seater roadster.

SPECIFICATION
Engine: Longitudinal, front, rear-wheel drive **Capacity:** 265cu. in. OHV V8
Bore/stroke: 3.75 × 3.00in. **Power (DIN/rpm):** 225bhp **Torque (DIN/rpm):** N/A
Fuel system/ignition: 2 four-barrel carburetors/mechanical **Transmission:** 4-speed manual, 2-speed Powerglide automatic
Front suspension: Unequal length A-arms, coil springs, anti-roll bars
Rear suspension: Live axle, leaf springs
Brakes: Drums front and rear **Wheels/tires:** N/A
Max. speed: 129mph (207kph) **0–60mph:** 7.3 sec

Earl hoped that his creation would sell for $1,850, around the price of a Chevy sedan. His enthusiasm carried enough weight for the management to give him carte blanche to undertake a full-blown but very secret development project. To keep costs down, Earl was told to raid the Chevy parts bin and so he had chief engineer Maurice Olley take the

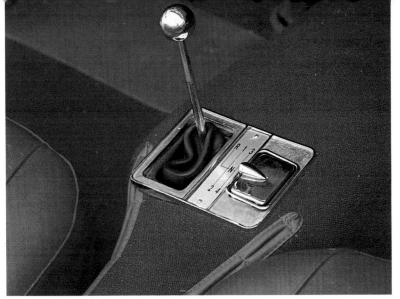

floorpan from a production sedan and reduce its wheelbase to 102 in. The production car had a more thoroughly developed chassis using an X-member frame with box-section side rails, outboard mounted rear leaf springs and a Hotchkiss drive. Weight distribution and handling were helped by siting the engine 13 in. further back in the chassis

than in other Chevys.

The dramatic and futuristic looking Corvette should have been a smash hit, but the early cars were plagued with troubles, some inherent design flaws, others due to inadequate production engineering. Performance from the 150bhp six-cylinder engine was uninspiring and assembly line problems with the complex body kept Corvette production to just 315 cars in 1953. The Corvette's saviors were Edward N. Cole, the new chief engineer, who installed a 30 lb lighter 195bhp V8 motor in the car, and Zora Arkus-Duntov who worked to improve the chassis. For all that, and a price cut, only 674 Corvettes were sold in 1955. GM were just about to write off the Corvette as a bad experience when Ford launched their Thunderbird. GM had to hold their ground and a stay of execution gave Harley Earl the chance he needed to redesign the Corvette. In an era where cars were becoming chrome embellished tasteless monstrosities, the 1956 Corvette was like a breath of fresh air. At last GM could justifiably claim that the Corvette was 'America's only true sports car'.

Without changing the 52/48 percent weight distribution,

Zora Arkus-Duntov managed another round of improvements in the suspension and steering and the superb 265cu.in. V8, previously an option, now became standard with 210bhp in normal or 225bhp in tuned form. Also standard was a close-ratio three-speed manual box. 0–60mph (0–96kph) took 7.5 seconds and top speed was 120mph (193kph). Boring out the engine to 283cu.in. for 1957, Chevy produced a range of five engines varying in tune from 220bhp to 283bhp. The most powerful version used the new Ramjet fuel-injection system which proved finnicky in service. Known as the 'fulie' among enthusiasts, this version would wipe the 0–60mph sprint in just 5.7 seconds and top out at 132mph (212kph). With the heavy duty suspension package, the Corvette became an out-of-the-box stock racer. Motor racing success now became a consistent part of the Corvette legend and when a car came ninth in the 1956

Sebring 12 Hours and others won or were highly placed in SCCA events, the Corvette had at last come of age. Sebring put the seal on GM's plastic baby as one of the world's finest sports cars, and sales took a dramatic turn for the better.

It is ironic that the launch of a competing product should give the Corvette the chance it needed to prove itself. The basic ingredient were there all along but the art of designing, packaging and marketing a car for a specific target audience was still young in the 1950s, and mistakes were made. As the Corvette slowly moved toward the plush GT concept it was to adopt later in life, the 1958 model, along with a very long stretch of highway, were immortalized in the TV series 'Route 66'.

Except for 1983, the Corvette has remained in constant production since it first appeared three decades earlier. A 1980s ad campaign trumpeted it as 'the heartbeat of America'. The legend goes on.

DE LA CHAPELLE BUGATTI T55

In 1976, a young entrepreneur by the name of Xavier de la Chapelle
set out to build a replica of his dream car, the 1931
Bugatti Type 55. With BMW mechanicals and a chassis developed
by an ex-Matra engineer, the de la Chapelle
Bugatti's pedigree is impeccable, more especially as it was
sanctioned by M. Hispano Bugatti, of the original Bugatti
family, and so can use the exalted name in its title. Although a replica,
the de la Chapelle car captures the spirit of the original perfectly.

SPECIFICATION

Engine: Longitudinal, front, rear-wheel drive **Capacity:** 2693cc
Bore/stroke: 84 × 81mm **Power (DIN/rpm):** 210bhp @ 6000rpm **Torque (DIN/rpm):** 177lb ft @ 4800rpm
Fuel system/ignition: Bosch Motronic/electronic **Transmission:** 5-speed manual
Front suspension: Double wishbone, coil springs, telescopic dampers, anti-roll bar
Rear suspension: Double wishbone, coil springs, four telescopic dampers, anti-roll bar
Brakes: Four-wheel disc, vented front and rear **Wheels/tires:** Alloy. 6J × 15in. 205/65VR15
Max. speed: 130mph (209kph) **0–60mph:** 6.8 sec

Replicas are all about recreating the look, feel and ambience of the original car as closely as possible. With a body made from glass-fiber rather than hand-beaten aluminum, it has a long bonnet with louvered side vents, sensuously curving wheel arches, two-tone paintwork and the distinctive eight-spoke wheels, all of them Bugatti hallmarks. Yes, the

wheels are smaller than they should be and the rubber around them much wider, but form follows function, and 210 Alpina–BMW bred horses could not keep their hooves on the ground any other way. That is the most powerful engine option, but you can have a plain BMW 2.5 liter 171bhp version if outright performance is not a priority.

The nature of the car's construction lends itself to a rigid center ladder chassis with tubular frame perimeter sections. The suspension is lightyears ahead of the original's but needs to be to contain the power and torque of the modern BMW engine while giving a quiet and supple ride. Penned by ex-race car designer Jacques Hubert and further developed by Group C engineer Philippe Beloou, the chassis uses double wishbone suspension at each corner with twin coils and dampers at the rear. Sophisticated geometry and anti-roll bar linkages ensure optimum handling characteristics.

As modern as it may be in its engineering, the de la Chapelle car is built carefully by craftsmen in the traditional way. This shows especially in the interior where well-padded seats covered with soft leather and a hand-polished walnut dashboard take center stage. This magnificent backdrop for the silkscreen printed instruments is not a veneer, but is carved from the solid. Even Rolls-Royce do not go this far! The instruments that sit square in the center wear black numerals on magnolia faces with the Bugatti, de la Chapelle and Jaeger logos below. Under the dashboard is the climate control panel with three hand-turned knobs that conjure up images of esoteric radio sets from the period. The only part of the replica that is not user friendly and thus truly traditional is the canvas top. If you are accustomed to the convenience of power tops that raise and lower in 30 seconds, you will definitely get wet in a sudden downpour.

People who love the style of the classic convertible but shun the shortcomings of running a period car may well find empathy with this dual character modern classic. When they visit the Brignais factory near Lyon, and take a test drive, they may well find that they have had the same dream as Xavier de la Chapelle.

DODGE VIPER

Every V8-powered sports car that has seen the light of day in the last twenty-five
years has been compared to the legendary AC Cobra.
But thanks to a daring move by Chrysler's Dodge division, the standard
bearing Cobra is now being challenged by a snake of a
different color. Enter the Viper. With 8.0 liters of V10 power, 400bhp
and 450lb ft of stump-pulling torque, this 1990's roadster
with the drop dead looks will get to 60mph in 4.6 seconds and top out at
167mph (268kph).

SPECIFICATION

Engine: Longitudinal, front, rear-wheel drive **Capacity:** 7997cc, V10
Bore/stroke: 102 × 99mm **Power (DIN/rpm):** 400bhp @ 4600rpm **Torque (DIN/rpm):** 450lb ft @ 3600rpm
Fuel system/ignition: Electronic fuel-injection/electronic ignition **Transmission:** 6-speed manual
Front suspension: Unequal length double wishbones, coils, anti-roll bar
Rear suspension: Unequal length double wishbones, coils, anti-roll bar
Brakes: Four-wheel disc, vented fronts with four-pot calipers **Wheels/tires:** Alloy. 10J × 17in. (F), 13J × 17in. (R) Michelin XGT2
Max. speed: 167mph (268kph) **0–60mph:** 4.6 sec

The story goes back to 1988 when a group of Chrysler executives including President, Bob Lutz, and Carroll Shelby sat down to talk about sports cars. The classic Cobra kept coming up in the conversation and the decision was taken to build a one-off concept car of a 1980's Cobra interpretation for the US motor show circuit the following year. Detroit, Chicago and New York. Public reaction to the Viper concept car at these shows was unprecedented. A public bored with dozens of unadventurous computer generated shopping cars was more than excited and the Chrysler offices were bombarded with letters. postcards and phone calls with more than a few people willing to write checks! It would have been easy to ignore all of this, especially as the world was entering the deepest recession since the 1930s, but Chrysler took the long-term view. In the meantime, having such a car in their model line up would do the company's image no harm at all.

The Viper's composite body panels are either bonded or bolted to a race car-style tubular steel frame to which the suspension is attached. Again in

typical race style, there are unequal length upper and lower wishbones with coil-over shocks at each corner. The rear arms have separate toe-links and there is an anti-roll bar at each end.

Chrysler-owned Lamborghini also played a role in the Viper's development. Lamborghini were given the task of converting the workaday iron engine from a forthcoming Chrysler truck project into an all-alloy masterpiece for the Viper RT/10, the car's official tag. So, in fact, the first ten or so blocks and heads were Italian-produced, coming from Lamborghini's headquarters at Sant'Agata Bolognese, near the city of Modena.

Some F1 cars have ten cylinders, so the Viper is exotic in its cylinder count and alloy block alone. The rest of the motor is classic Detroit small block with two valves per cylinder, pushrods and hydraulic lifters. The tremendous torque output required ZF to build a special gearbox. This six-speeder has a direct-drive fourth with the last two gears overdriven. 70mph (112kph)) in sixth is barely 650rpm above idle!

The Viper personifies the old adage 'there's no substitute for cubic inches'. The effect is all the stronger because the weight is just 3380lb, giving a power-to-weight ratio of 263bhp/ton. Feed in the throttle and the torque hits the road like a Tomahawk cruise missile. Unlike the Cobra, the Viper's chassis was designed to take this power from the start and so traction is good

considering the forces at work. Most supercars accelerate hard to, say, 100mph and then just gather speed. The immense reserves in the V10 belie the laws of physics and the feel of real acceleration does not abate till reaching a speed of around 140mph (225kph).

The steering is quick and accurate but does not have the intimate feel of a Ferrari 512TR or Porsche 911. Grip is enormous

with just a trace of understeer. The car is mostly neutral through bends, which gives you the option of steering with your right foot. In the wet, things can get interesting! Equally impressive is the ride. Mid-corner bumps have little effect on the car's line and a long trip underlines how hugely comfortable the suspension is. Body control is magnificent.

For less than the price of an entry level Ferrari 348 or Porsche Carrera 2, the Dodge Viper comprehensively outguns most of the big Italian supercars in usable performance and overall abilities. And it looks a million dollars too. With this combination, at last the AC Cobra has met its match. The New Kid on the Block is the Top Gun from Dodge City.

FERRARI MONDIAL CABRIOLET

Tradition says Ferraris should be two-seaters. This is the reason that
Ferraris with back seats have never sold well.
In recent years the four-seat 412, the only front-engined car in
Maranello's range, has also been its slowest seller.
The sensational new 456 may, in retrospect, see a change
to that and if it does more people might also
consider the other Ferrari with a back seat – the
underrated Mondial.

SPECIFICATION

Engine: Longitudinal, mid, rear-wheel drive   **Capacity:** 3405cc V8 DOHC, four valves/cylinder
Bore/stroke: 85 × 75mm   **Power (DIN/rpm):** 300bhp @ 7200rpm   **Torque (DIN/rpm):** 237.2lb ft @ 4200rpm
Fuel system/ignition: Electronic fuel-injection/ignition   **Transmission:** 5-speed manual
Front suspension: Double wishbone, coils, anti-roll bar, anti-dive geometry, electronically controlled gas dampers
Rear suspension: Double wishbone, coils, anti-roll bar, electronically controlled gas dampers
Brakes: Four-wheel disc, vented front and rear   **Wheels/tires:** Alloy. 7J × 16in. (F), 8J × 16in. (R), 205/55ZR16 (F), 225/55ZR16 (R)
Max. speed: 158mph (254kph)   **0–60mph:** 6.2 sec

Introduced in 1980 in 3.0 liter 240bhp form, the four-cam V8 powered Mondial quattrovalvole was flawed in the eyes of purists by having a back seat, and to everyone else because it was not fast enough. Ferrari partially redressed the balance in 1985 by bumping displacement to 3.2 liters which added 30bhp and 33lb ft of torque. But the real renaissance

of the Mondial in fixed and drop-head forms did not come till December 1989 when the present 3.4 liter engine with a healthy 300bhp and 237.2lb ft of torque arrived along with power-assisted steering and electronically adjustable Bilstein dampers for the suspension. At the same time, the new powertrain was turned to sit longitudinally rather than transversely in the chassis and positioned lower to improve handling, equalize the exhaust pipe runs and make service access easier.

Accompanying these mechanical changes, the interior of the Mondial t, as the car is now known, was totally revised. The new seats are deeper and more comfortable, the instruments and steering wheel in line with current Ferrari practise. But for all that, the 1985 3.0 liter shown here was not unsound ergonomically. Compared to the 308/328 two-seaters, the Mondial has a much better driving position than is normally found in Italian cars. The steering wheel and gear lever fall naturally to hand and the foot controls are medium weighted and full of feel. This synergy in the control input and feedback relationship makes the Mondial an easy and very sweet car to drive.

Typical Ferrari tubular frame construction makes for a rigid car. In Cabriolet form, the Mondial is no Mercedes-Benz SL, but considering it has a long 104.3 inch wheelbase, it is better than many decapitated hot hatches in the area of scuttle shake.

Designed by Pininfarina, the Mondial's styling has been

criticized for lacking the beauty of line more openly manifest in two-seaters from the same stable. Perhaps this is unfair, for within the constraints of the brief the car has turned out rather well. Certainly the Cabriolet looks sensational with the top down and from a rear three-quarter angle it bears strong resemblance to a 308/328 Cabriolet, if ever such a car had been made. And as with all Ferraris, the angels are in the details. When you visually dissect parts of the composition, you feel excitement rising as you interpret, understand and even feel the design process that makes a Ferrari 'grow', first in line and form and then in detail before your eyes.

If, as a fan of older Ferraris, you were to criticize the Mondial or indeed any modern V8-engined Ferrari at all, it would be in the area of the engine note. Since Ferraris forsook carburetors for fuel-injection to meet emission and noise legislation, their aural stimulation has been much less appealing. A modern Ferrari lacks the inspirational sucking and gurgling of multiple Weber carburetors, thrashing of timing chains and the howl of a throaty exhaust. Now they just whine. The upside though is a much more tractible and totally untemperamental power unit that will pull smoothly from barely above idle in fifth gear.

Marry that to a balanced and comfortable chassis that feels user-friendly even at speed on a sodden race track where its two-seater sisters feel nervous and spin happy and you have a Ferrari that is fun to drive and practical to use on a daily basis.

FORD MUSTANG CONVERTIBLE

In 1965, Ford had a runaway success on its hands. The Mustang was selling in huge numbers: over a million copies before its first birthday. Ford had created the pony car segment and other manufacturers were forced to follow or be left behind. But more than just being popular or affordable the Mustang was an interesting car. An aspirational vehicle, it could be a compact luxury car with economy as a six-cylinder, power with a V8 or brute power in Shelby Mustang form. The convertible version was just plain sexy.

SPECIFICATION
Engine: Longitudinal, front, rear-wheel drive **Capacity:** 260cu. in. V8 OHV
Bore/stroke: 3.80 × 2.87 in. **Power (DIN/rpm):** 164bhp @ 4,400rpm **Torque (DIN/rpm):** N/A
Fuel system/ignition: 2 × Autolite carburetors/mechanical **Transmission:** 3-speed manual or Cruise-O-Matic automatic
Front suspension: Independent, wishbones, coils, telescopic dampers
Rear suspension: Live axle, leaf springs, telescopic dampers
Brakes: Four-wheel drum **Wheels/tires:** Steel. 5J × 14in. 6.95 × 14 crossplies
Max. speed: N/A **0–60mph:** 11.2 sec

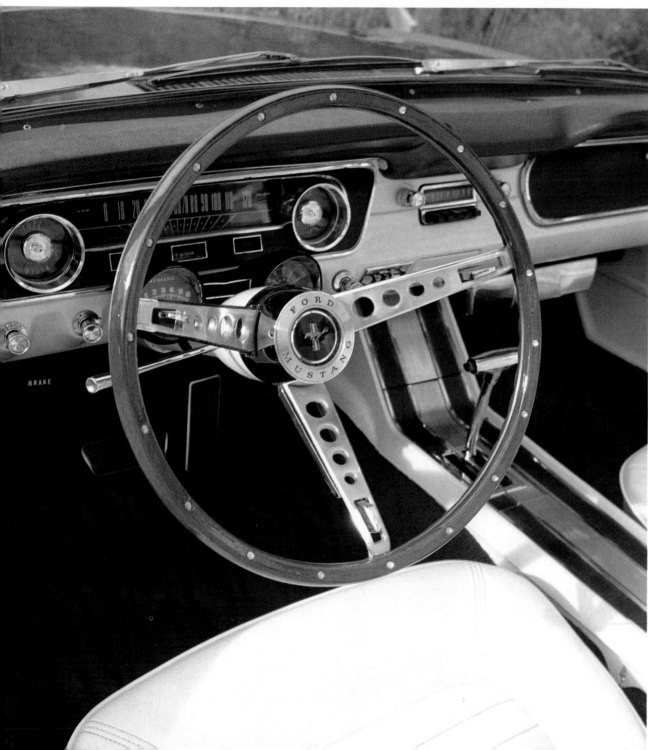

Ford came up with a two-page color advertisement for the car's launch which read, 'Mustang has the look, the fire, the flavor of the great European road cars, yet it's as American as its name... and as practical as its price.' Seldom has a truer word been spoken in the cause of product promotion, and the Mustang appealed to singles and young married couples, people who would have been called yuppies two decades later.

The man to take the lion's share of the credit for the Mustang was Lee Iacocca. Appointed to the post of Ford Division general manager in 1960 at the age of thirty-five, he was sure that there was a niche in the market for a sporty, low-cost compact. It was a car that Iacocca thought he might want himself. At the time, Fords were named after birds, hence the Thunderbird and Falcon. But John Conley of Ford's ad agency was by now into horses. Colt, Bronco, Pinto and Maverick came to mind, but Mustang, which conjured up images of cowboys, prairies and the romantic Wild West was a natural. It was catchy, evocative, exciting and all-American. The wild, free-spirited horse that was to become a familiar chrome badge on the grille of the Mustang was carved out of mahogany as a template and a legend was born.

In 1964, you could buy the Mustang as a 2 + 2 coupé, hardtop or ragtop. The open Mustang sold for just $2,614. Buyers choose the V8 engine option on a three-to-one basis and tended to load the car from the long options list that

covered virtually every aspect of the car. Thus, the mundane Falcon suspension could be improved with a handling package. If the 101hp 170cu.in. six-cylinder engine which would give 30mpg was insufficient, you could order a 260cu.in. V8 with 164bhp or a 289cu.in. V8 with 195bhp. If that was still inadequate, a four-barrel carburetor gave 210bhp. Finally, for real power freaks, an HP version gave 271bhp. This engine also had 312lb ft of torque helped by a 10.7:1 high-compression head, high-lift cam, solid lifters, flowed induction and exhaust systems, and other improvements. The puny base engine soon gave way to a 200cu.in. 120bhp six which gave quite respectable performance. The chief mechanical improvement offered in 1965 was the optional front disc brakes which were well worth the extra on V8 cars as the front drum brakes were not noted for their stopping power or fade resistance.

In straight-line go, a properly optioned Mustang would show a clean pair of heels to most of the imported sports cars like MGs and Triumphs. *Motor Trend* achieved a 0–60mph (96kph) time of 7.6 seconds for the HP version which would reach 123mph (197kph). But it was not until the facelifted, arguably more cluttered 1968 Mustang with its 427cu.in. big-block engine rated at 390bph came along that Ford truly had a Mustang in the supercar league. This car would sprint to 60mph in 6.0 seconds but its handling was not brilliant, being nose heavy and prone to power oversteer. As a car to drive, the Mustang was nothing special. But its size, style and the options list which allowed you to personalize it to your needs for reasonable money offered buyers just what they wanted after a generation of variations on mundane family sedans. The Mustang started the pony car revolution which was imitated not just by other American manufacturers but by car makers around the world. The European Ford Capri, Japan's Toyota Celica and all the small coupés that have followed owe their inspiration to the Ford Mustang.

FORD THUNDERBIRD

In American Indian folklore, the Thunderbird symbolizes power,
swiftness and prosperity. With a base sticker price of
$2,695 when it was launched in 1955, the Ford Thunderbird
did not demand too much prosperity from its
owners. But the 292cu. in. V8 Mercury engine delivered
202bhp and greater swiftness that the earlier
six-cylinder versions of the Chevy Corvette from which it was
designed to win customers.

SPECIFICATION

Engine: Longitudinal, front, rear-wheel drive **Capacity:** 312cu. in. V8
Bore/stroke: 3.80 × 3.44 in. **Power (DIN/rpm):** 245bhp @ 4500rpm **Torque (DIN/rpm):** 332lb ft @ 3200rpm
Fuel system/ignition: Four-barrel carburetor/mechanical **Transmission:** Fordomatic automatic, three-speed
Front suspension: Double wishbones, coil springs, telescopic dampers
Rear suspension: Live axle, leaf springs, telescopic dampers
Brakes: Drums front and rear **Wheels/tires:** N/A
Max. speed: 119mph (190kph) **0–60mph:** 8.5 sec

Ironically, it was Ford's Thunderbird that gave the ailing Corvette its second lease of life. Poor sales of the underdeveloped Corvette had put its future on the line. It was the threat of losing sales to the new Thunderbird that made Chevrolet take a long, hard look at their own car. Like the Corvette, the Thunderbird was also built on a 102in. wheelbase, but was a larger, more square rigged car, more the open two-door tourer than the roadster-like Corvette. Tagged as a 'personal' car rather than a sports car, the T-Bird would seat three providing the person in the middle had short legs!

First shown at the 1954 Detroit Auto Show as a wooden mock-up, the T-Bird was a practical luxury car with a steel body, a power-operated option for its roll-up side windows, a snug powered soft-top, lift-off hardtop or both. To keep costs down, the car used many proprietary Ford parts, but the rakish long hood and short deck of the body conjured up images of the classic Lincoln Continental from the decade before. Penned by the young

stylist, Bill Boyer, the T-Bird was smooth, elegant, clearly Ford.

With looks, quality and power on its side, the T-Bird drew the crowds to Ford show-rooms. In 1955, the year it was launched , it outsold the revised Corvette 24 to 1! Seemingly Ford could do no wrong, so for 1956 (the model shown here), rather than risk messing things up with a restyle, they con-centrated on improving the strengths of the car. A 312cu.in. engine option with 225bhp was added, the ride improved with softer suspension. Aesthetic changes found the spare wheel mounted on the outside which also liberated more trunk space, while the attractive hardtop now had the option of portholes. The T-Bird was easy to drive with good handling aided by a steering ratio that gave 3.5 turns lock-to-lock with or without power-assist. The 312cu.in. 225bhp version took 10.2 seconds to get to 60mph; top speed was 116mph (186kph).

Development of the T-Bird progressed very quickly, but by now Ford was looking for volume which they could only get with four-seater cars. Thus 1957 was the last model year for the T-Bird and this was arguably the best of the lot. 285bhp was available from a

version of the 312cu.in. engine with twin four-barrel carburetors. For real speed freaks, 208 special supercharged T-Birds were built with 340bhp, but these were mainly used in motorsport, where the car had limited success. The 1957 model year facelift brought a more prominent fender/grille, longer rear deck that returned the spare wheel to inside the trunk, modest tail-fins and larger rear lights. The long production run that year produced 21,380 cars, about 50 percent more than each of the previous two model years. It was also the first American two-seater to sell in really high numbers. Acknowledged as the definitive T-Bird, the '57 is the most sought after model.

Apart from being a really worthy car, the stylish Thunderbird was a commercial success which gave large manufacturers the confidence they needed to embark on other two-seater touring and sports cars projects in the ensuing years. There was a time lapse of several years though, during which manufacturers made a run of uninspiring four-seater two-and four-door cars. Then happily, the spirit of the original T-Bird was reincarnated in the Ford Mustang.

HONDA BEAT

It is a stylish and modern mid-engined two-seater that attracts
as much attention as a Ferrari and comes complete
with air-conditioning, electric windows and a built-in
CD-based stereo package in its racy
looking cabin. But it is narrower than a Mini and just
a smidgen longer. The Honda Beat could
only be created by the Japanese, the masters
of miniaturization.

SPECIFICATION
Engine: Transverse, mid-engine, rear-wheel drive   **Capacity:** 656cc, three-cylinders in-line
Bore/stroke: 66 × 64mm   **Power (DIN/rpm):** 64bhp @ 8100rpm   **Torque (DIN/rpm):** 44lb ft @ 7000rpm
Fuel system/ignition: Electronic fuel-injection and ignition   **Transmission:** 5-speed manual
Front suspension: MacPherson strut, lower arms, anti-roll bar
Rear suspension: MacPherson strut, radius rod trailing links, twin lateral links
Brakes: Four-wheel disc   **Wheels/tires:** Steel. 4.5J × 13in. (F), 5J × 14in. (R), 155/65HR13 (F), 165/60HR14 (R)
Max. speed: 87mph (139kph)   **0–60mph:** 9.8 sec

Powered by a 646cc engine, the Beat was made to fit into a segment of the Japanese market called 'microcars'. In Japan, parking spaces are at a premium and taxes accrue in proportion to the size of a vehicle. Microcars are the answer to this fixed cost dilemma and have to exhibit extreme technological innovation and density to give buyers as much if not more excitement in their driving than they would get from full-sized cars. That the manufacturers have identified the possibility of making such small cars chic designer accessories and also fun to drive is to their credit, and once again underlines the slickness, awareness and inventiveness of Japan Inc.

The Honda Beat is cute, but it is also very well proportioned. Look at a photograph or even the real car without any common object around to use as a size reference, and you could be fooled into thinking it was a full-sized sports car like a Mazda MX-5. Approach the Beat and you find yourself looking down on a dinky little machine barely two sizes up from a fun fair bumper car.

If you are tall, you will climb in and perhaps laugh as you almost peer over rather than through the windscreen. But the Beat is every bit the serious sports car. Its cabin underlines that fact. You will either love or hate the zebra patterned cloth trim on the seats and the matching floor mats, but you will also admire the attention to detail on the instrument pack which is mounted in a pod on the steering column as on a motorcycle. Believe it or not, there is even a driver's side airbag available as an option, while side-intrusion bars in the doors are standard.

Packed as it is with so much in the way of goodies, the one thing the Beat is short on is space for luggage. City hopper it may be but the Beat is no shopping car. A third of its diminutive trunk is taken up by the battery, leaving just about enough room for an attaché

case. A squashy bag for a weekend away is probably asking too much, and anything larger is undoubtedly asking the impossible.

If the Beat has one problem, it is weight. It is not heavy in absolute terms but for a car of its size, 1,676lb (760kg) makes it 200lb (90kg) greater in avoirdupois than an original 1960s Lotus Elan! The weight is not due so much to the gadgets as a very strong structure designed to all but eliminate scuttle shake and give the suspension a firm platform from which to work.

The little three-cylinder engine manages to muster 64bhp at 8100rpm, but the peak torque of 44 ft at 7000rpm is not so clever. Even to achieve this, the motor has had to be given four-valves-per-cylinder, operated by a SOHC and rocker arms, electronic fuel-injection and one throttle butterfly per cylinder. A close ratio five-speed gear box helps and the

Beat will get to 60mph (96kph) in 9.8 seconds and eventually reach something close to a satisfactory 90mph (144kph).

On the open road, the Beat has more going for it than many full-sized sportsters. It is lively, sophisticated and as much fun as a barrel of monkeys. Ride quality is not bad even if it can get a bit lively at times. But the little engine is sharp, responsive and allows you to play the serious racer, thriving on high rpm and making a lovely off-beat noise while doing it.

One of the most affordable sports cars made in recent years, the Honda Beat challenged its makers' ingenuity to come up with a car that could give a high level of driver satisfaction in a package the size of a golf-caddy. Honda succeeded admirably in their goals and the followers-on have not quite managed to surpass this level of innovation. As often happens, original is best.

JANKEL TEMPEST

On 13 April 1992, just over a year after the first car was built, a Jankel
Tempest entered the *Guinness Book of Records* by
blasting aside the 3.98 second 0–60mph benchmark for standard
production cars set by the Ferrari F40 in February
1989. Driven by Mark Hargreaves, the supercharged 6.3 liter
Tempest launched down the strip at Millbrook
Proving Ground to clock a best run of 3.89 seconds and
thus snatch the record.

SPECIFICATION

Engine: Longitudinal, front, rear-wheel drive **Capacity:** 6.3 liters, V8
Bore/stroke: N/A **Power (DIN/rpm):** 610bhp @ 5300rpm **Torque (DIN/rpm):** 608lb ft @3800rpm
Fuel system/ignition: Electronic fuel-injection and ignition. Supercharged with water injection and liquid charge intercooler
Transmission: 6-speed manual **Front suspension:** Independent. Transverse monoleaf spring, anti-roll bar, electronic damper control
Rear suspension: Electronic. Transverse monoleaf spring, anti-roll bar, electronic damper control.
Brakes: Four-wheel disc, vented with four-pot calipers front and rear **Wheels/tires:** Alloy. 9.5J × 17in 275/40ZR17 (F), 315/35ZR17 (R)
Goodyear Eagle GCS **Max. speed:** 200mph (321kph) **0–60mph:** 3.5 sec

By the time the first anniversary of the record came around, Robert Jankel had sold thirty-two bespoke Tempests, quite an achievement for a £90,000 car in the depths of a world-wide recession. But it would appear that the Tempest is able to infuse would-be customers with the same excitement that drove its maker to relentlessly fashion the concept from the seed of an idea into brutally powerful reality.

The proud owner of an original Jaguar E-Type V12 and a Proteus D-Type replica, Jankel had for some years hankered after a car in a similar mold, but more modern and practical. Designing and building special cars like stretched and armored Rolls-Royces for wealthy individuals and heads of state for a living, Jankel knew that making a totally new car was very expensive, so he had to find a car on which to base his concept of a powerful, front-engined, rear-driven convertible supercar. This car would have to be very fast out of the box so that it would not require total re-engineering. The L98 Corvette fitted this profile exactly. Even so, the Corvette undergoes a far-reaching metamorphosis to transform it into a Tempest. At least half the car is shed straight away including the handsome glass-fiber bodyshell which Jankel mimics in ultra-light carbon-Kevlar, but with substantially revised nose and tail treatment.

The standard engine is replaced by a 6.3 liter blueprinted, supercharged and water-injected V8 built by Los Angeles-based Traco, whose reputation in the US racing scene is second to none. A Vorteck-R supercharger provides up to 10psi of boost through a gas-flowed induction system and the inlet air temperature is dropped by a liquid intercooling system with a surface area as large as the stock Corvette's radiator! Sophisticated digital motor electronics look after the fueling and ignition and the high pressure water injection system operates when the knock sensor detects the approach of detonation. When the Tempest took the 0–60mph (0–96kph) record, it had 530bhp and 608lb ft of torque. With the Vorteck-R blower and other revisions, the engine now makes 610bhp at 5300rpm and 608lb ft of torque at 3800rpm. There is over 400lb ft of torque available just off idle speed.

The Corvette chassis has carbon-fiber filament-wound monoleaf springs at each end. In the Tempest, these are damped by Bilstein gas shocks which work with the factory electronically adjustable ride control. The suspension is rose jointed. Huge racing brakes with four-pot calipers linked to the Bosch ABS system easily stop the Tempest from a 200mph charge. 60–0mph takes just 119 ft (36 m.). The

interior is stock Corvette but retrimmed in the finest leather which can be anything from soft doe-skin to buffalo hide.

The Tempest goes like the wind it is named after. Punch the throttle in fifth gear at 80mph (128kph) and you generate the sort of thrust you would experience in a fast 2.0 liter car accelerating hard in second gear from 30mph (48kph). All the while, the sophisticated Corvette traction control system ensures that the awesome power is translated to forward momentum rather than melting the tires or snapping the car sideways. So the Tempest is not only easy to drive, it is easy to drive fast. The mark of a true supercar.

LORENZ & RANKL
SILVER FALCON

The shape is familiar and yet not ; the proportions are right
and the detailing exquisite. There are hints of the
Alfa Spider, Ferrari 250, E-Type Jaguar and even Mercedes 300SL
in its styling. This car may take its cue from these and other
famous classics, but despite clear 1950s and 1960s inspiration, the
Lorenz & Rankl is not a replica or a pastiche of a particular
period car. The concept of Peter Lorenz, the Silver Falcon is very much
a sports car of the 1980s.

SPECIFICATION
Engine: Longitudinal, front, rear-wheel drive **Capacity:** 4973cc, V8
Bore/stroke: 96.5 × 85mm **Power (DIN/rpm):** 265bhp @ 5200rpm **Torque (DIN/rpm):** 298lb ft @ 4000rpm
Fuel system/ignition: Bosch mechanical/electronic fuel-injection. Electronic ignition
Transmission: 4-speed automatic **Front suspension:** Double wishbones, coils, adjustable tie-rods, anti-roll bar
Rear suspension: Independent, trailing arms, coil springs, anti-roll bar **Brakes:** Four-wheel disc. Vented front
Wheels/tires: Borrani wire wheels. 7J × 15in. (F), 8J × 15in. (R); 225/60VR15. Goodyear Eagle NCT
Max. speed: 145mph (233kph) **0–60mph:** 5.7 sec

Recognized by the German transport authorities as a manufacturer, Lorenz & Rankl have a short but glorious history. Founder Peter Lorenz is a graduate of Munich and Dortmund universities in mechanical and automotive engineering. He joined Ford in 1955 and was pilot plant manager for Ford of Europe by the time he left in 1970. After a stint with Teves, he 'retired' from the industry in 1977 to work for himself.

It is every car designer's dream to make his own sports car and Lorenz was to achieve this through initially building a Cobra replica using Mercedes-Benz engine and suspension parts hung on his own tubular chassis design. Commercial success with this gave him a proven platform on which to base the Silver Falcon, a car that was truly his own.

The Silver Falcon took nine months over 1984–5 to develop. Under the hand-formed aluminum body sits a massive tubular steel chassis designed to work with Mercedes V8 power. This can be anything from the old 5.0 liter 231 bhp W126 S-Class motor to the current 326bhp 32-valve 500SL engine. The engine sits behind the front

suspension, quite far back in the chassis, giving a favorable weight distribution. Basically a tubular ladder design, the stainless steel chassis incorporates a few unique ideas like the use of the huge circular rear members as carriers for the twin exhausts that eventually emerge as pairs. The top of an open car must be simple to operate and look an integral part of the car's design. The Silver Falcon's soft top is all of these, and just for the record, the front windscreen and quarter lights are Alfa Spider. Another practical plus is a surprisingly spacious trunk. Lining the comfortable cabin with its cosy bucket seats is hardwearing German leather with deep pile carpet underfoot.

From this luxurious vantage point, you turn the key in the ignition and experience the lusty whoof of a big V8 awakening from its snooze. A low pitched rumbling follows and is matched by a deep burble from the four exhaust pipes behind your head. Prod the throttle and the massive torque just off idle rocks the car on its firm suspension.

The engine in this example is out of a W126 500SE and with over 240bhp and bags of torque in a car weighing about as much as a VW Golf, the Silver Falcon rockets out of bends and pulverises the straights. Throttle response is instant, the acceleration almost neck snapping. You can waft along on the fat torque curve, but prod the Silver Falcon and she turns into a silver arrow in the best German *Silberpfiel* tradition.

For all her obvious performance capabilities, the Silver Falcon does not strike you as a car for tearing around in. She may not bear a Ferrari or Alfa legend on her flanks, but the Silver Falcon can hold her head up high in any company. Lorenz & Rankl is a contemporary marque, the Silver Falcon is a classic sports car of the future.

LYNX JAGUAR XK-SS

Back in the 1950s, Formula One single-seaters were clearly bred just for the
track, but the line drawn between sports cars that
raced at international level and ones you could buy and drive to
the shops was very thin indeed. You could almost see the
three-times Le Mans winning D-Type Jaguar as a daily driver because
the roadgoing XK-SS version differed only by having a proper
windscreen, side screens, nearside
door, better trim, canvas top and no tail-fin.

SPECIFICATION
Engine: Longitudinal, front, rear-wheel drive   **Capacity:** 3781cc, six-cylinders in-line, DOHC
Bore/stroke: 87 × 106mm   **Power (DIN/rpm):** 285bhp   **Torque (DIN/rpm):** N/A
Fuel system/ignition: 3 twin-choke Weber 45DCOE carburetors   **Transmission:** 4-speed manual
Front suspension: Double wishbones, torsion bars, telescopic dampers
Rear suspension: Independent. Transverse tubular and trailing links. Twin coil springs and telescopic dampers each side
Brakes: Four-wheel disc, inboard at rear   **Wheels/tires:** Alloy. 5.5J × 16in. 6.00 L16 Dunlop racing crossplies
Max. speed: 153mph (246kph)   **0–60mph:** 5.3 sec

Jaguar's original game plan was to build 100 D-Types between 1954 and 1957 for Le Mans homologation purposes. Ultimately only eighty-seven cars were made: six works racers, fifty-four production cars, eleven long-nose versions and sixteen XK-SS road cars. The balance was lost in a fire which destroyed a third of the Jaguar plant, but by then it hardly mattered, for the D-Type had served its purpose and Jaguar resorted to converting the remaining D-Types into XK-SSs.

It is not just the glory and imagery conjured up by the Le Mans 24-Hours that makes the D-Type probably the most replicated sports car after the AC Cobra. It is actually a very inspiring car to drive. The Lynx XK-SS replica, based on an E-Type chassis, is in some ways even better than the original live-axled car. Apart from being

exquisitely hand-fashioned from aluminum sheet, as it should be for £80,000, it gets its power down better and has a more comfortable ride.

And what of the driving? On a still day, you can hear the Jaguar coming for miles! The ride is firm but supple and through fast bends the gracefully curved Jaguar grips well considering its cross-ply tires. Handling is superb and very entertaining with this much power, but you have to remember that the racing cars of the 1950s had less grip than today's average saloon car.

Ironically given its age, the Jaguar D-Type/XK-SS, a supercar of the 1950s, is a much more practical and usable proposition than many of today's mid-engined sports cars. Apart from creating interest rather than envy in onlookers, it is compact, light, powerful and easy to place on a country road, and is as direct, tight and communicative as one could wish for in a road car. The Lynx XK-SS has a top speed of 153mph (246kph), will pass 60mph (96kph) in 5.3 seconds and get to the magic ton in 13.1 seconds from rest.

LOTUS ELAN SE

The *Oxford English Dictionary* defines 'elan' as 'vivacity' or 'life force',
an apt name for a small, swift sports car designed to inspire.
Colin Chapman's original Elan from the 1960s was undoubtedly the
epitome of its name. Certainly Lotus could find no better
appellation to bestow upon the small, swift sports car that emerged
from their factory in 1990. The sadness is that, at the end
of 1992, the decision was taken to cease production of a car that
was already being called a classic.

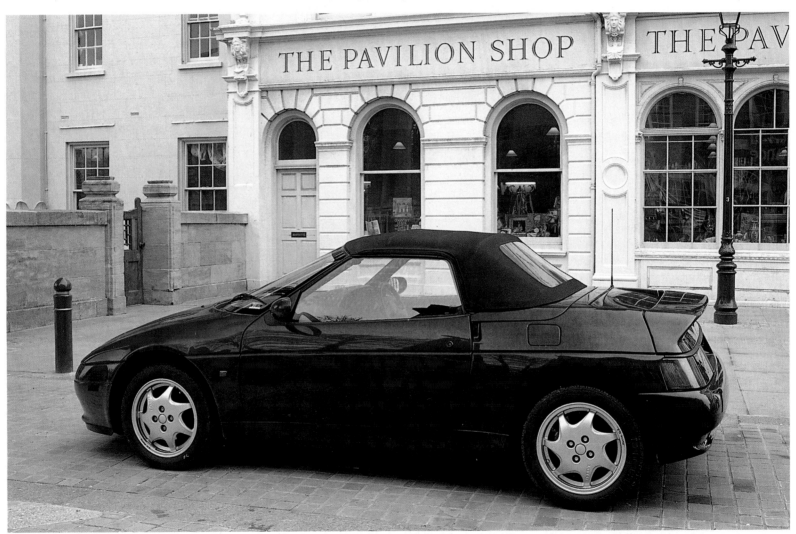

SPECIFICATION
Engine: Transverse, front, front-wheel drive **Capacity:** 1588cc, four-cylinders in-line, four valves/cylinder, DOHC
Bore/stroke: 80 × 79mm **Power (DIN/rpm):** 165bhp @ 6600rpm **Torque (DIN/rpm):** 148lb ft @ 4200rpm
Fuel system/ignition: Electronic fuel-injection and ignition. IHI turbocharger **Transmission:** 5-speed manual
Front suspension: Independent. MacPherson struts, lower wishbones, anti-roll bar
Rear suspension: Independent, MacPherson struts, lower wishbones, anti-roll bar
Brakes: Four-wheel disc. Vented front and rear. ABS **Wheels/tires:** Alloy. 6.5J × 15in. 205/50ZR15
Max. speed: 135mph (217kph) **0–60mph:** 6.5 sec

Ironically, while history is littered with the wreckage of cars that have been ahead of their time, the second bearer of the Lotus Elan name was actually too late, introduced at too high a price into a shrinking market. For when it was announced that no more Elans would be made, it seemed that, suddenly, everyone wanted one. But despite speculation that production might be resumed at some point in the future, the bare truth is that the Isuzu engine which the Elan uses has now ceased production and the cost to homologate its successor or even the Toyota alternative which was originally considered, would make the car commercially uneconomical. So in the years to come, the Elan will be a rare

sight and thus has already achieved classic status.

The Elan set new standards of handling and roadholding for front-wheel-drive cars. It must have been a tough decision at Lotus's headquarters at Hethel to abandon the traditional rear-drive layout, but when they did they set about perfecting their new charge with a vengeance. A front-wheel-drive car with a turbocharged 1.5 liter 16-valve four-cylinder engine gives the drivetrain and steering rather a lot to think about when it has to corner and steer at the same time. But Lotus engineers practically re-invented front-drive suspension geometry, and the Elan shows only a minute trace of torque steer even when being driven in anger on bumpy country roads. Only in the wet does loss of traction in aggressive standing starts manifest a wiggle through the superb power-assisted steering. On small roads, the Elan is in its element: it is nimble, fluid and very, very fast, qualities that leave supercars with double its power floundering in its wake.

All this ability did not come easy though and the Elan gave

its engineers many sleepless nights. There is no single magic ingredient. Rather, the Elan's suspension is an amalgam of many carefully designed components and carefully calculated geometry that work harmoniously together to achieve their design objective. Significant is the alloy 'raft' on which each front suspension assembly is mounted and which in turn is connected to the chassis. This allows the wide-based wishbones to use stiff bushes for geometrical purity while the softer bushings that mount the rafts to the chassis absorb road shock and noise.

This accounts for the good ride that accompanies the Elan's fine handling. Another aid to handling is an extremely rigid structure on which the non-stressed RRIM plastic body panels are mounted.

From its cosy leather covered cockpit, the Elan offers a terrific view of the road over its short, sloping nose. The Isuzu engine does not make any inspiring noises, in fact it is rather bland, but it is a very effective power unit, offering good throttle response and bundles of mid-range torque. In a car this light without the corrupting influence of rear-wheel-drive power losses, the Elan puts most of its 165 horses to good use. 0–60mph (96kph) comes up in 6.5 seconds and top speed is 135mph (217kph).

Introduced into a speculators' market where cars were traded as commodities , the Elan was not as fully appreciated as Lotus intended. Sadly, only after production has ceased are people beginning to realize just what a great contribution the Elan has made.

MAZDA MX-5 MIATA

Each decade of automobile development produces at least one car that finely
balances the vital ingredients of styling, performance, price, image
and potential so well that it becomes an instant classic. A sports car with these
qualities spans cultural boundaries best because it appeals directly
to the emotions. Such a car is the Mazda MX-5. Known as the Miata in the USA,
the MX-5 was born in Mazda's Californian planning office in
the mid-1980s when Mazda planned a small sports car to fill the gap
left by the RX-7.

SPECIFICATION
Engine: Longitudinal, front, rear-wheel drive **Capacity:** 1597cc, four-cylinders in-line, four valves/cylinder
Bore/stroke: 78 × 83.6mm **Power (DIN/rpm):** 116bhp @ 6500rpm **Torque (DIN/rpm):** 100lb ft @5500rpm
Fuel system/ignition: Electronic fuel-injection and ignition **Transmission:** 5-speed manual
Front suspension: Independent, unequal length double wishbones, coils, telescopic dampers, anti-roll bar
Rear suspension: Independent, unequal length double wishbones, coil, telescopic dampers, anti-roll bar
Brakes: Four-wheel disc **Wheels/tires:** Alloy. 5.5J × 14in.185/60HR14
Max. speed: 116mph (186kph) **0−60mph:** 8.6 sec

Mazda were looking for a high-tech solution, but Robert L. Hall, a former journalist, proposed a simpler and more classic design based on passion and emotion.

Initially, the Japanese were dumbfounded that an American should suggest they take two steps backwards in the evolutionary process of the sports car in order to go forwards. But as the team worked through the concept of a pure bred sports car, they too became smitten with the idea. Under the heading 'oneness between man and horse', six areas of a sports car's subjective performance – handling, driving performance, touch, visual perception, acoustic perception and direct brake feel – were analysed. These categories were then broken down into more specific areas. Visual characteristic like a power bulge in the bonnet and a large chrome tailpipe or subjective characteristics like suitable kickback in the steering and a firm, well weighted brake pedal.

Despite its back-to-basic approach, Mazda did not actually set out to produce an old-style sports car. On the contrary, the Miata is designed and built using the latest

technology available. Thus some very advanced thinking lies cheek by jowl with basic design ideas. While the suspension is traditional race car style unequal length double wishbones and coil springs at each corner, there is a form of a passive rear-end steer using bushes tuned to provide self-correcting toe-geometry under high lateral g-force loads. Another innovation is an alloy framework that bolts over the propshaft to keep the transmission and rear differential in a rigid relationship.

With just 1.6 liters offering 115bhp and 100lb ft of torque, the MX-5 had to be light. Babyface tips the scales at 2128lb (990kg) distributed 52/48 percent front/rear. With two on board, this becomes the ideal 50/50. This allows an 8.6 second 0–60mph (0–96kph) spring and ultimately 116mph (186kph). When it comes to turning and stopping, the little Mazda shines. Rack and pinion steering with optional power-assistance sees to that. An all-disc brake system offers strong and progressive retardation and can haul the car down from 60mph in exactly 148 ft (45m.).

Forget stopping for a moment and just go! That is what the Mazda is good at. Slip behind the wheel and you will not find any gimmicky distractions like trip computers or digital instruments. The interior design is instead overtly simple and uses the curved theme of the car and its various design elements to create a dialogue that is repeated in the form of the instrument pod, center console and the molded recesses containing the

105

switchgear in the dash. That same circular and oval theme carries on throughout the car to unify it in an almost organic way.

You soon find yourself using the slick short-throw gearbox just for the tactile pleasure its precision gives. You slow unnecessarily to feel the sharp throttle response and hear the growl of the little twin-cam singing toward the red-line again before you snap the short

gear lever across the gate. This, without doubt, is automotive poetry in motion.

The MX-5 combines classic feel and response with modern design, attention to detail and reliability. It is highly addictive, utterly seductive, and yet cost effective. The incarnation of painless sports car ownership at its very best, the MX-5 Miata will go down in history as the renaissance of the affordable sports car.

MERCEDES-BENZ SL

The Mercedes-Benz sports car lineage that began in 1952 with Rudolph
Uhlenhaut's famous 300SL Gullwing and its Cabriolet sister
has always shown purity of form, a vital ingredient if a design is
to resist erosion by the sands of time. Current design
chief, Bruno Sacco, has proven his mastery of pure forms with
the latest incarnation of the SL theme, a wedge-shaped
roadster that looks right from every angle, top up or down and
with its hardtop in place.

SPECIFICATION

Engine: Longitudinal, front, rear-wheel drive **Capacity:** 4973cc, V8, four valves/cylinder
Bore/stroke: 96.5 × 85mm **Power (DIN/rpm):** 326bhp @ 5500rpm **Torque (DIN/rpm):** 332lb ft @ 4000rpm
Fuel system/ignition: Bosch mechanical/electronic fuel-injection. Electronic ignition **Transmission:** 4-speed automatic
Front suspension: MacPherson strut, lower arms, anti-roll bar
Rear suspension: Independent, multi-link, anti-roll bar
Brakes: Four-wheel disc. Vented. ABS **Wheels/tires:** Alloy. 8J × 16in. 225/55ZR16
Max. speed: 155mph (250kph) **0–60mph:** 6.1 sec

It has been said that the technologically dense SL is over-complex and over-weight for its size. But this is an impression gleaned more by the bank vault-like construction and fine finish of the car than by reference to the scales. The reality is that modern materials have added greater strength while enabling the new car to be 12 percent lighter than its predecessor.

High-tech is certainly evident in the plethora of electronically controlled on-board systems. You expect electric windows, mirrors and central locking in most cars these days. In the SL, add ABS, ASR anti-skid, adaptive damping and a host of other features such as the roll-over bar which flicks up into its locked position in just 0.3 of a second should the sensors detect that a wheel has left the ground. The structure of the SL is immensely strong.

Mercedes takes great pride in showing how you can jack up one corner of the car and still open and close the doors or operate the soft-top perfectly. The German magazine, *Auto Motor & Sport*, put a brace of open cars on a torsional stiffness test machine and pronounced the SL the world's stiffest open car.

On the road, the feeling you get is the same as driving any fixed head Mercedes – that the car is carved from the solid. Suspension comfort is first class, and so it should be in a car that will whisk you across continents in comfort and style. How fast you can go is dictated by the engine you have chosen. The entry level SL has the 180bhp 12-valve straight-six, but the most popular model is the 220bhp 300SL-24. Both these engines are to be replaced by a 3.2 liter 220bhp engine which offers a useful increase in torque. At introduction, the fastest SL was the 5.0 liter 32-valve V8 powered 500SL which achieved 326bhp with the aid of variable valve timing. Recently, this has been upstaged by the 394bhp V12 engined 600SL which has a 6.1 second 0–60mph (0–96kph) capability. As with all powerful

German production cars, the SL is electronically speed limited to 155mph (250kph).

Driving an SL gives you a tremendous sense of well-being. Pull the thick and heavy door shut and the solid thunk is reassuring. Cossetted in the deeply cushioned leather covered seat you notice the solidly constructed cabin architecture with walnut wood inserts on the center console and in the door panels. Some may consider a Mercedes-Benz

interior sterile, but you will find no finer finish in a production car.

On balance, the 500SL is still the optimum model. The V12 car is not significantly quicker and its greater weight in the nose cannot do the handling balance any good. At the other end of the scale, the 300SL-24 performs briskly and the 320SL should be even better. But the distant rumble of a well-tuned V8 takes a lot of beating. It is also a question of torque and,

with 346lb ft, the V8 has more than enough grunt to make the Mercedes roadster a horizon chaser. In design, finish, performance and image, there are few cars that can compete with the Mercedes-Benz SL. If it has a character flaw, it is the electronic wizardry which tames driver excesses. It is nice that the SL's poise and road manners should remain unflappable, but it also makes it too perfect to be an enthusiast's sports car.

MORGAN PLUS 8

Call it old-fashioned, call it impractical, but the car that Morgan enthusiasts the
world over lust after is a 'contemporary classic', a 30-year-old
design whose apparent flaws are looked upon as facets of its character. Morgan
owners are fanatics first and sports car lovers next. More
than just car makers, the Morgan Motor Company, situated at the foot of the
Malvern Hills in the west of England, is an institution, founded
in 1909 by H. F. S. Morgan. Guided by his son and grandson, the present firm
has gone from strength to strength.

SPECIFICATION

Engine: Longitudinal, front, rear-wheel drive **Capacity:** 3947cc, V8
Bore/stroke: 94 × 71.1mm **Power (DIN/rpm):** 190bhp @ 4750rpm **Torque (DIN/rpm):** 220lb ft @ 2600rpm
Fuel system/ignition: Electronic fuel-injection and ignition **Transmission:** 5-speed manual
Front suspension: Independent. Sliding pillars, coils, telescopic dampers
Rear suspension: Live axle, leaf springs, telescopic dampers
Brakes: Disc front, drum rear **Wheels/tires:** Alloy 6.5J ×15in. 205/60VR15
Max. speed: 130mph (209kph) **0–60mph:** 5.6 sec

There are many replicas of 1930s style cars on the market and these are largely built by modern methods, and often with GRP bodies. Morgan make their 1930s design from wood, steel and aluminum using 1930s methods. For any other company, this *modus operandi* would be commercial suicide, but Morgan's fortunes are as much about the attitude of their customers as the company's planning. In today's hard business world where sales and marketing are ruled by supply and demand, any other company would not have survived. The typical Morgan buyer is not considering a sports car: he or she wants a Morgan. And so it is business as usual with the waiting list for your bespoke car still over five years.

It would be wrong to say that nothing has changed over the years, however, for significant, albeit slow development work has been done to the suspension to help the car cope with the powerful Rover V8 engines that found their way into the classic shape in 1968. And, of course, as Morgans are technically 'new' production cars, they have to meet the exhaust emission laws of the various countries in which they are sold. So three years ago, the Plus 8 gained a fully catalysed 3.9 liter version of the venerable all-alloy V8 as installed in the Range Rover. Homologated for the US market, this is the cleanest and most powerful engine ever fitted to a production Morgan.

190bhp is not a lot in supercar terms , but a Plus 8 weighs under 2000lb (907kg). Helped by 220lb ft of torque at

just 2600rpm, it takes only 7.6 seconds to accelerate from 50 to 70mph (80–112kph) in top, a test of flexibility that cannot be matched by the vastly more powerful Ferrari Testarossa.

Amid the striking lack of clear identities in modern cars, the individuality and purity of a Morgan is pleasing. The overall shape is pure 1930s: the long bonnet, short tail and sweeping mudguards that run from the front bumper into the running boards and then the rear mudguards. All these body panels are hand fashioned either in steel or aluminum according to the customer's wishes. At the front, the multi-slatted radiator grille is lovingly pieced together by a master craftsman. All these metal parts find their final resting place on a traditional timber frame chassis that concedes only to modern methods for locking out the environment. You can have three different engines in your Morgan: a Ford CVH, a Rover 2.0 liter 16-valve or the Rover V8. You can also have a longer wheelbase car with a rear seat if you need to carry the children. But the purist version is most definitely the two-seater Plus 8.

You must take the Morgan for what it is rather than trying to judge it by modern standards. If you would buy a car because you enjoy looking at it, appreciate its craftsmanship and like listening to the deep throaty rumble of its torquey V8, then you may be pleasantly surprised when you allow the Morgan to show you its own very special interpretation of genuine old-fashioned motoring. But be warned: Morgan ownership can become an obsession.

117

PEGASO Z-103

Pegaso is the Spanish name for Pegasus, the winged horse of mythology.
The name on the badge is as fitting a symbol on this car as
the shape of the Italian *cavallino* is on a Ferrari. But today the Pegaso badge
appears only on trucks sold in Europe; few people remember
the marque which only turned out 125 sports cars between 1951 and 1958.
But there were many body styles, some by Touring of Milan, and
production of the most elegant Pegaso of all, the Z-103,
only ran to six cars.

SPECIFICATION

Engine: Longitudinal, front, rear-wheel drive **Capacity:** 3948cc, V8
Bore/stroke: 94 × 71.1mm **Power (DIN/rpm):** 170bhp @ 4750rpm **Torque (DIN/rpm):** N/A
Fuel system/ignition: Electronic fuel-injection/ignition **Transmission:** 5-speed manual, rear-mounted
Front suspension: Double wishbone, coils, telescopic dampers
Rear suspension: De Dion axle, Watts linkage, coils, telescopic dampers
Brakes: Four-wheel disc. Vented fronts **Wheels/tires:** Wire wheels. 5J × 15in. Avon Turbospeed crossplies
Max. speed: 120mph (193kph) **0–60mph:** 8.5 sec

The notion of a Pegaso sports car was conceived in 1945 when Wilfredo Ricart joined Pegaso as chief engineer. Coming straight from Alfa Romeo, he brought with him the dream of an exclusive Spanish car to rival the great Italian marques: high performance coupés and convertibles with sophisticated mechanicals clad in elegant bodywork designed and crafted by top Italian coachbuilders. When Ricart retired in 1958, Pegaso returned to the exclusive manufacture of commercials.

Then in 1992 came the Barcelona Olympics, with car maker SEAT as one of the big sponsors. And out of that came the revival of the Pegaso by ENASA-Pegaso and the Spanish

Government.

The Spanish had approached International Automotive Design (IAD) of Worthing, England, in mid-1988. The largest automotive consultancy group in the world, IAD were asked to replicate the Z-103, and evolve it into a limited production car that would meet current emission and safety regulations. Modern parts were used where copies of the originals would have been too costly. In place of the 3.1 liter four-cam V8 motor was an easy to maintain 170bhp alloy 3.9 liter Rover V8. Instead of hand-formed aluminum bodywork, the IAD car uses a seam-welded steel shell attached to an all-new but conceptually similar steel chassis rust-proofed to current standards. Suspension is recalibrated Alfa Romeo GTV6.

IAD's Pegaso is a journey back in time to an era when sports cars were pure in line and purpose. This is no recreation of a cheap roadster though. It is the thorough development of a car that in its day stood proudly alongside the best from Alfa Romeo, Ferrari and Lancia.

120

PORSCHE 911 CARRERA 2

After an unsuccessful attempt with the 928 in 1978, Porsche stopped trying to
kill their best-selling 911. Thirty years old in 1993, making it the
longest lived sports car in history, the Porsche 911 has become an
institution, an icon and even an objet d'art among
die-hard fans. Each generation of 911 has got better and better,
and as if finally to endorse the concept that
a skeptic once described as 'the triumph of development over engineering'
the 911 replacement will also be rear-engined.

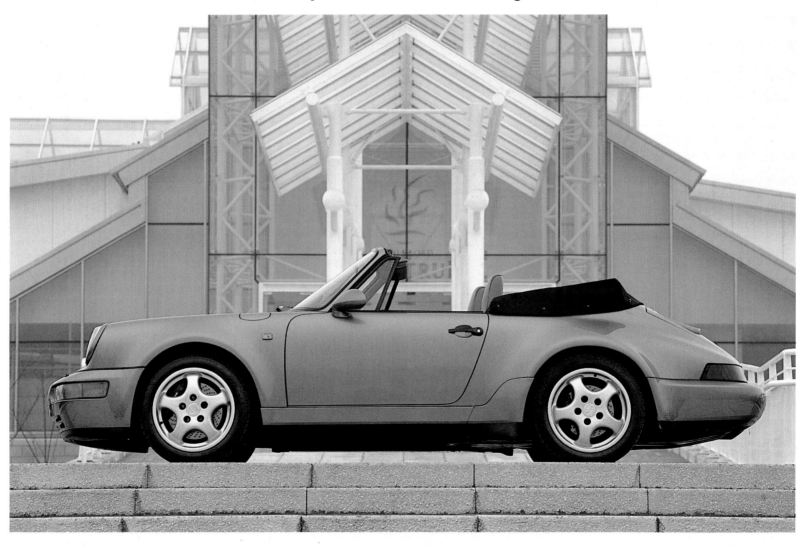

SPECIFICATION

Engine: Longitudinal, rear, rear-wheel drive **Capacity:** 3600cc, flat-six, air-cooled, twin-plug
Bore/stroke: 100 × 76.4mm **Power (DIN/rpm):** 250bhp @ 6100rpm **Torque (DIN/rpm):** 229lb ft @ 4800rpm
Fuel system/ignition: Bosch Motronic fuel-injection/ignition **Transmission:** 5-speed manual or 4-speed Tiptronic
Front suspension: MacPherson struts, coils, telescopic dampers, anti-roll bar
Rear suspension: Semi-trailing arms, coils, telescopic dampers, anti-roll bar
Brakes: Four-wheel disc. Vented front and rear. ABS **Wheels/tires:** Alloy. 8J × 17in. (F), 9J × 17in. (R), 205/50ZR17 (F), 255/40ZR17 (R)
Max. speed: 157mph (252kph) **0–60mph:** 5.5 sec

Originally conceived as a coupé, the 911's first open variant was launched in August 1967 as a Targa with a folding rear screen and removable roof panel. The first full cabriolet version was not to arrive for another sixteen years though, coinciding with the final production year of the 911SC whose 3.0 liter engine was 50 percent larger than the first 911's.

In the mid-1980s, responding to a market hungry for more and more exotic variations of the basic theme, Porsche produced a version of the Carrera Coupé called Super Sport Equipment. This gave the car the wider wheel arches of the fashionable Turbo as well as its suspension and brakes, but with power coming from the 231bhp 3.2 liter naturally aspirated Carrera engine. An SSE version of the Carrera Targa and Cabriolet followed, and a Turbo Cabriolet appeared in 1988. As this era of the 911 drew to a close, Porsche announced a Speedster version as the last variation on this theme. This arrived just as the speculative classic car market – which had convinced a lot of people that they could get rich quick – self-destructed.

As with most cars that lost

their roofs late in life, the open 911 lacks the structural rigidity of its fixed-head counterpart. Particularly in wide-bodied form, these early open 911s suffered from scuttle shake and suspension geometry changes under high cornering loads. But when Porsche transformed the Type 901/930 cars into the current 964/965 models in 1989, they gave them an all-new floorpan and heavily revised structure that took into account not only the latest crash regulations, but also the Targa and Cabriolet versions. Thus, all open Carrera 2/4 cars are purpose-built and not merely decapitated coupés. The ultimate test of this rigidity comes in the form of the Carrera 2 Cabriolet Turbo Look.

The 3.6 liter engine in the Carrera 2/4 cars musters 250bhp at 6100rpm. Peak torque is 229lb ft at 4800rpm, but 80 percent of this is present from a tad under 2000rpm. The throttle response of this wonderfully charismatic flat-six motor is so much crisper than any turbocharged engine that the car is better placed to take advantage of overtaking situations and holds the advantage on tight, twisty roads where instant response is required. With the weight of the engine over their rear wheels, all 911s have terrific traction out of corners in the dry, and with the Turbo chassis, the Cabriolet Turbo Look car has more grip and brakes than it needs, making it very swift cross country.

But what is most impressive about this new Cabriolet is the rigidity of the structure. You can brake deep into corners, accelerate hard out of them or simply drive briskly down bumpy roads and experience little in the way of scuttle shake. Roof up or down, the car feels rock-solid, tight and all of a piece. With ABS coupled to the huge Turbo vented discs, the 911 Turbo Look probably has the best brakes of any road car. Acceleration is fierce, handling well sorted and the perfectly judged power-steering allows you to make light work of town driving.

The power roof is one of the best around. With its locking mechanism concealed in the top of the windscreen frame,

the system works at the touch of a button when the engine is off but the ignition on. It takes just 20 seconds for the roof to unlock, gracefully sweep over your head and fold neatly into the rear compartment. Then you just have to add the canvas cover which only takes a minute. Al fresco, the musical wail of the 911's flat-six in full cry takes on an extra dimension. Its sound and response is half the appeal of this car; half the reason that the forthcoming 911 replacement will also have a flat-six engine in the back.

ROLLS-ROYCE CORNICHE

1993 was the 25th anniversary of the Rolls-Royce Corniche convertible.
To mark the event, the factory made twenty-five numbered
cars, all in Ming blue with blue-piped magnolia hide. In time to come, these
cars will no doubt become collectors' items, but
Rolls-Royce and Bentley motor cars, the most luxurious hand-crafted
conveyances in the world, are made to be used and enjoyed.
A convertible Rolls-Royce or Bentley is the ultimate symbol of pomp
and circumstance.

SPECIFICATION

Engine: Longitudinal, front, rear-wheel drive **Capacity:** 6750cc, V8
Bore/stroke: N/A **Power (DIN/rpm):** 226bhp **Torque (DIN/rpm):** 340lb ft
Fuel system/ignition: Bosch K-Motronic fuel-injection/ignition **Transmission:** 4-speed automatic
Front suspension: Independent. Coils, lower wishbones, anti-roll bar, automatic variable ride control
Rear suspension: Independent, semi-trailing arms, coils, anti-roll bar, automatic variable ride control
Brakes: Four-wheel disc. Vented in front **Wheels/tires:** Alloy. 7J × 15in. 235/70R15
Max. speed: 126mph (202kph) **0–60mph:** 10.4 sec

In its latest guise, the Corniche IV has a redesigned power-operated soft-top with a heated glass rear screen, automatic ride control which adapts the suspension to driving conditions and ABS brakes. So under the skin, the car is pretty much state-of-the-art. What has not changed in twenty-five years, apart from the bumpers, is one single line

on the classic and elegant Mulliner Park Ward hand-built coachwork.

The Corniche was designed by Bill Allen, a Rolls-Royce man since 1935. He created the shape single-handedly in just six weeks using a few bits of balsa and half-inch ply, a few pounds of styling clay, dozens of hand-cut paper templates and a five-foot long drawing-board. Although the job was finished in 1963, the car did not go into production until five years later. Named after the Grande Corniche, the high road between Nice and Monaco, near where Sir Henry Royce, the company's founder, had his winter home, the Corniche is the epitome of the lifestyle led by the rich and famous who inhabit this part of the south of France.

Rolls-Royce Motors have always kept the power and torque outputs of their cars deeply shrouded in mystery. If the line of questioning veers that way, a company spokesman is trained to deflect an inquiry with the word 'adequate'. What is no secret though is the fact that the engine is a 90° V8 displacing 6.75 liters, fueled by Bosch K-Motronic electronic fuel-injection/ignition and coupled to a four-speed automatic gearbox. Although the latest Rolls-Royce and Bentley saloons now have their gear selector lever in the center console, the Corniche retains the steering column-mounted system of yore.

If you like your home comforts, you will find no other car interior to equal that of a Rolls-Royce. The seats are deep and sumptuous. Pull the heavy

door open and the smell of the Connolly leather begins to seduce your olfactory senses even before you move to step inside. Comfortably seated behind the long prow with the 'spirit of ecstasy' and edge of the bonnet forming a convincing illusion of a near horizon, you cannot help but feel good. The inlaid burr walnut is hand-crafted to perfection and punctuated only by neat shut lines for the glove box and cutouts for the instruments, air vents and controls. The vents and door catches are thickly chromed and gleam at you proudly as they catch the light. Even after months or years of ownership, people are still moved to run their hands over the smooth paintwork, open the door just to catch a whiff of the atmosphere and touch the wood and leather inside.

But is the Corniche a car to enjoy driving? Older versions were very smooth but wallowed alarmingly when pushed into corners. With the automatic ride control system, a computer linked to sensors all round the car constantly monitors the suspension. Push the car into a bend and in a millisecond the suspension has tightened up to give near sports car response. Cruise along the highway and it all settles down to cossett you in supreme comfort. All the time, the powerful V8 is just a distant whisper, the unseen mailed fist in a velvet glove always ready to whisk you away in the twinkling of an eye.

It is hard to judge a Rolls-Royce, and especially a Corniche, by the standards of other cars. Forget the fact that it only does ten miles to the gallon driven briskly; forget the fact that it is hard to park in congested cities. Such mundane facts of life are beyond the cares of people for whom the Rolls-Royce Corniche is not just a car but a way of life.

TVR GRIFFITH

TVR are pastmasters of the traditional rugged long bonnet, short-tailed
sports car. But their stunning Griffith, classical in
proportions yet modern in detail, is far from being a melting-pot
of styling idioms. Through the careful use
of much original thought in the execution and finishing
of its simple and elegant form, the Griffith
manages to stand out within its genre as arguably the sports
car for the 1990s.

SPECIFICATION
Engine: Longitudinal, front, rear-wheel drive **Capacity:** 3950cc, V8
Bore/stroke: 94 × 71mm **Power (DIN/rpm):** 240bhp @ 5750rpm **Torque (DIN/rpm):** 275lb ft @ 4200rpm
Fuel system/ignition: Electronic fuel-injection/ignition **Transmission:** 5-speed manual
Front suspension: Unequal length double wishbones, coils, telescopic dampers, anti-roll bar
Rear suspension: Unequal length double wishbones, coils, telescopic dampers, anti-roll bar
Brakes: Four-wheel disc. Vented front **Wheels/tires:** Alloy. 7J × 15in. (F), 7.5J ×16in. (R), 205/60ZR15 (F),
225/55ZR16 (R) **Max. speed:** 152mph (244kph) **0–60mph:** 4.9 sec

Some of the detail work is clever, the rest simply wonderful. The neat little chromed door handles in the finger-sized sculpted cut-outs atop the door trailing edges, for instance, show that the Italians do not have the monopoly on style. More obvious are the compound curves that form the bonnet airflow egress route and the sculpted rebates behind the front wings. This exquisite detailing compliments the sensuously curved body panels, setting up an eloquent dialogue between form and detail. Enter the car through the wide doors and you find an elegantly curved burr walnut dashboard that merges into the inner door panels and an organically shaped center console to continue the homogenous styling ethic. Ensconsed in the feel and rich aroma of quality hide, you quickly feel at home.

As graceful to look at as a ballerina, the Griffith is as tough under its glass-smooth bodyshell as an Olympic weightlifter. The GRP bodyshell is riveted, glued and bolted to a stout tubular steel frame backbone chassis that is phosphated, polyester coated and guaranteed for ten years.

133

Most TVR models have a successful racing pedigree, and the Griffith's chassis benefits from a wealth of motorsport development with the similar Tuscan. That is just as well, for the car, initially available with the Rover V8 in 240bhp 4.0 liter or 295bhp 4.3 liter form, is being relaunched with TVR's own engine, the AJP V8, which promises 360bhp in basic tune! Set well back in the long nose to help weight distribution, this engine placement creates a similar configuration to a mid-engined race car like a Ford GT40, but in reverse. Just hearing the TVR blow past you in full cry will make you want to drive it. The deep V8 burble and shattering growl shout power with a capital 'P', and although it makes all the noises of a traditional American muscle car, the lithe TVR is as taut and sinewy as a greyhound.

In driving effort, the TVR is definitely old school of thought, and more recent Griffiths have had their front tires reduced in size from 215/50ZR15 to 205/60ZR15 to lessen low speed steering effort. Neither are the clutch and gearshift for the wimps of this world. But master the driving dynamics, and you are rewarded with real pleasure. Blip the throttle. There is a 'whump' from the double-barreled exhaust behind your head. Engage first, let in the progressive clutch and accelerate away, and a wave of torque hits you in the back as the car storms off the line with that gritty, offbeat rumble from up front that can only come from a finely fettled V8. The ride is firm and well controlled and the car turns into bends crisply with well-bred poise.

TVR are a remarkable company who produce several interesting variations on a basic theme. If they have mastered the art of the 1960s-style sports car with their V8S, then the Griffith is a strong argument for the title of 1990s equivalent. It is best though to forget trying to pigeon-hole the Griffith and simply appreciate it for what it is – a piece of modern sculpture that goes very fast and makes a nice noise!

VENTURI TRANSCUP CABRIOLET

Nearly a decade after its Paris Salon debut, the Charles Godfroy designed Venturi coupé still looks fresh and modern and easy on the eye: good design will always endure the test of time. But the chic coupé and its Transcup Cabriolet sister had more than just good looks. Venturi chairman Claude Poiraud was serious about his car matching the dynamic abilities of Ferrari and Porsche and so hired acclaimed Group C race designer Philippe Beloou to pen the Venturi's chassis.

SPECIFICATION

Engine: Longitudinal, mid, rear-wheel drive   **Capacity:** 2458cc, V6 turbocharged, inter-cooled
Bore/stroke: 91 × 63mm   **Power (DIN/rpm):** 200bhp @ 5750rpm   **Torque (DIN/rpm):** 210lb ft @2500rpm
Fuel system/ignition: Electronic fuel-injection/ignition   **Transmission:** 5-speed manual
Front suspension: double wishbones, coils, telescopic dampers, anti-roll bar
Rear suspension: Independent. Multi-link. Coil, telescopic dampers, anti-roll bar
Brakes: Four-wheel disc. Vented front and rear.   **Wheels/tires:** Alloy. 7.5J × 16in. (F), 9J ×16in. (R), 205/55ZR16 (F), 245/45ZR16 (R)
Max. speed: 153mph (246kph)   **0–60mph:** 6.7 sec

Originally launched under the MVS (Manufacturer de Voitures de Sport) name, and later backed by Xavier de la Chapelle's Primwest France consortium, this suave French sports car has now adopted its model designation for its corporate banner.

The constraint of low production costs on the chassis inspired commonality of parts such as non-handed front lower wishbones, identical Rose joints all round and four 11.0-inch ventilated discs within a chassis that is as symmetrical as possible. The suspension is attached to a sheet-steel tub chassis built around a central backbone, the perfect structure on which to mount the glass-fiber shell. The Cabriolet chassis is further reinforced with longitudinal steel members in the sill areas, but unlike most open cars the Transcup Cabriolet is actually 60lb (27.3kg) lighter than its hardtop sister. Roof up, the drag factor is an identical 0.31.

The Venturi comes with a choice of two power units, both from the same source. Based on the Renault Alpine GTA V6 Turbo, they come in 2.5 and 2.8 liter form, but the Cabriolet can only be had with the former. Even so, 200bhp and 210.4lb ft of torque is not to be scoffed at. It is enough to launch the Cabriolet to 60mph (96kph) in 6.7 seconds, and beyond that the 0.31 drag factor it shares with the coupé helps take it on to a 153mph (246kph) top speed.

And you do it all in supreme comfort. The leather and walnut cabin of the Venturi is tasteful, opulent and beautifully finished and gives

away nothing to hand-made English aristocrats like Aston Martin. Despite knobs, switches, heater controls and vents sourced from the Renault parts bin, the fascia is both cohesive and convincing.

Far from being a decapitated coupé, the Transcup Cabriolet is an individual and versatile model in its own right. Soft-top cars have always been a security risk and detachable hardtops are inconvenient to stow and transport. The Venturi not only solves both problems but also offers a total of four different configurations to suit the needs of the occupants.

With the electrically operated glass rear screen and the two hardtop panels in place, the car is effectively a coupé. With the air-conditioning going, it could cope with the heat of downtown Dallas in summer. Turn up the heater and an Alpine snow storm outside is only a minor nuisance. If driver or passenger want fresh air, either or both targa panels can be removed and stowed away. The car can then be driven like a targa. Finally, at the touch of a button, the rear screen drops into a hidden compartment in the rear deck, creating a full convertible.

Fully closed, the Venturi is a refined high speed cruiser. Al fresco, the noises you normally do not hear come to the fore. With no Gallic or Latin temperament, the Venturi power unit is silky smooth, but can now be heard uttering its primal howl overlaid by the V6 exhaust burble and the turbo's whistle. Taut and composed even over cobbled French roads, the chassis gets better as you go faster. Turn-in is sharp and precise, its breeding shining through strongly the more you ask of it. Throughout all this, there is nary a trace of scuttleshake. No other supercar can stake this claim, proving that a rigid backbone chassis is the best base for a convertible.

Cruise on the autobahns at three-figure speeds or trickle around town in air-conditioned bliss. Then drop the top and drive hard down your favorite country road. Dress up for the theater and dinner with your companion. The Venturi Transcup Cabriolet will handle all these tasks admirably. More than that, the Venturi has created its own brand of cachet To have achieved this without the heritage and resources of Ferrari or Porsche is more credit due to the Venturi team.

VW GOLF GTI CABRIOLET

Enthusiasm is infectious. While putting the finishing touches to VW's Golf
project in 1974, a handful of engineers in the prototype
department secretly worked on a 'Sport Golf' out of hours. They had
no idea at the time just how positive their management
would be toward the car, and VW in turn had no inkling that the Golf GTI,
as the production model was dubbed, would not only
become an international cult car but also give birth to a whole
new market segment.

SPECIFICATION

Engine: Transverse, front, front-wheel drive **Capacity:** 1781cc in-line four
Bore/stroke: 81 × 86.4mm **Power (DIN/rpm):** 112bhp @ 5800rpm **Torque (DIN/rpm):** 112lb ft @ 3500rpm
Fuel system/ignition: Bosch K-Jetronic fuel-injection **Transmission:** 5-speed manual
Front suspension: MacPherson strut, lower arms, anti-roll bar
Rear suspension: Torsion beam rear axle, semi-trailing arms, struts, anti-roll bar
Brakes: Vented front disc, rear drum **Wheels/tires:** Alloy. 6J × 15in. 195/50VR15
Max. speed: 108mph (173kph) **0–60mph:** 9.5 sec

If the Golf GTI started the hot hatchback craze, it was also the progenitor of yet another niche market product, the cabriolet based on production hatchbacks. After the sales success of the classic Karmann-built VW Beetle, it was logical that a soft-top Golf should also be made. Karmann were asked to prototype the car in 1976, and the Golf Cabriolet made its public debut at the Geneva Show three years later.

Cutting the roof off a monocoque bodyshell seriously compromises the structure, so Karmann added cross-members and sill reinforcements to the decapitated structure. If you peer under the car, you can see these longitudinal members running the length of the car between the wheel arches. A roll-over bar mates to both the stiffened sills and the car's sheet metal and a cross-member under the dashboard further braces the structure. Clever use is made of a rectangular sheet metal box both to provide rear structural support and form the luggage compartment.

Karmann made sure that their folding top was a work of art in itself. With a substantial steel frame, this double layered

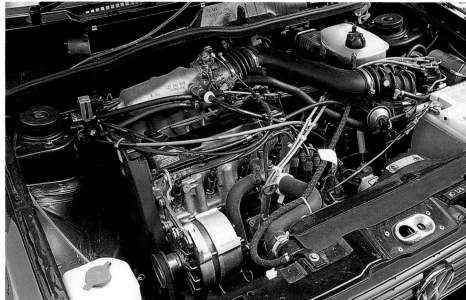

hood even has a glass rear window with electric de-mister. Secured by an adjustable catch at each end of the windscreen frame, the whole soft-top simply folds back behind the rear seat and can be neatly protected by a separate canvas cover. The manual top takes under a minute to raise or lower, while cars made after 1989 had the luxury of a power-operated top.

Making the Golf Cabriolet acceptably rigid created a weight penalty, however, and the basic car ended up 300lb (136 kg) heavier than the hatchback with a high proportion of that weight carried in the rear. Suspension settings were changed to cope and of course performance suffered. Even so, 0–60mph (0–96kph) in 9.5 seconds with a 108mph (173kph) top speed from a 112bhp 1.8 liter engine is respectable.

Launched in carburetor GL and fuel-injected GLi form, the Golf Cabriolet quickly developed its cult status and the latter was rebadged a GTI.

In the mid-1980s, the designer versions started to roll off the assembly lines in Osnabruck. An all-white version limited edition came first and was so popular that a second batch had to be built. VW then introduced a mix and match system whereby you could tailor the colors of the body, roof and interior to your individual taste. More limited editions followed in 1991 with the Rivage and Sportline being the luxury and sporty versions available in the UK with the Clipper replacing the original carburetor GL. For 1993, the final production year of the Mk 1 Golf floorpan Cabriolet, the special editions available in Europe were the Toscana, Acapulco, Classicline and Sportline, all with different equipment, colors and trim to emphasize their respective images. In catalysed form, the fuel-injected engine now had just 98bhp.

In 1993, the Golf Cabriolet jumped straight from Mk1 to Mk 3 in terms of the hatchback floorpan it was built on, but

even though it was thirteen years old and trailed newer rivals in grip and trunk space, the Golf could still hold its own in areas of build quality and driving pleasure. The VW has always been smooth and poised, with safe and progressive handling.

When you drive a Golf Cabriolet, you feel you are in a car with an air of class that puts it above newer, technically more advanced rivals. There is a totally homogenous quality feel to this car which makes it easy to understand why the Golf GTI hatchback it is based on quickly became accepted by both the rich and not so rich as the one small car you really had to be seen in.